WHAT VEGANS EAT
EASY VEGAN

WHAT VEGANS EAT

EASY VEGAN

BRETT COBLEY

HarperCollins*Publishers*

HarperCollins*Publishers*
1 London Bridge Street
London SE1 9GF

HarperCollins*Publishers*
1st Floor, Watermarque Building, Ringsend Road
Dublin 4, Ireland

www.harpercollins.co.uk

First published by HarperCollins*Publishers* 2021

1 3 5 7 9 10 8 6 4 2

Text © Brett Cobley 2021
Photography © Howard Shooter 2021

Brett Cobley asserts the moral right to be identified as the author of this work

A catalogue record of this book is available from the British Library

ISBN 978-0-00-844447-1

Food styling: Denise Smart

Printed and bound by GPS Group

MIX
Paper from
responsible sources
FSC™ C007454

FSC™ is a non-profit international organisation established to promote the
responsible management of the world's forests. Products carrying the FSC
label are independently certified to assure consumers that they come from
forests that are managed to meet the social, economic and ecological needs
of present and future generations, and other controlled sources.

Find out more about HarperCollins and the environment at
www.harpercollins.co.uk/green

I dedicate this book to my darling Tebogo; you are my inspiration and my compass. I wouldn't have been able to do it without you.

CONTENTS

INTRODUCTION

My story

I grew up lucky enough to make peanut butter cookies with my nan (see page 152). I licked the spoon and the bowl, then got to see the joy on my family's face as they bit into homemade cookies. I was hooked! Cooking food has always been a way for me to bring joy and connection to people I love. When I had my eyes opened to the state of the present-day food system – the 1.3 billion tons of food wasted each year, the 72 billion land animals slaughtered for food, and the 800 million starving people throughout the world – I realised that the way we eat needs to change. The decision to go vegan was not only for the animals but for humans. Going vegan is the biggest individual change we can make to positively impact the planet and reduce our environmental footprint.

In May 2016 I set up my Instagram account to share pictures and recipes of what I was creating in the kitchen each day. This was my way of showing people how I was transitioning to a vegan lifestyle and how they could have a positive impact on their health, the environment and animals, yet still create amazing, tasty food in their kitchen.

Since my first book, *What Vegans Eat*, I have seen vegan and low-waste movements flourish. I want to do more to help and hope this book can give you the inspiration you need to get you in the kitchen, reduce your impact on the planet and give you a sense of pride and fulfilment.

The state of play

The world can be a confusing place. When people hear 'vegan', 'low waste' or 'homemade', they can often feel overwhelmed. These terms can sound restrictive, expensive and complicated. However, I am here to guide you. I am going to talk you through it and offer tips, tricks and recipes that will help you to:

- **SAVE MONEY**
- **REDUCE YOUR IMPACT ON THE PLANET**
- **CREATE TASTY FOOD FOR ALL**

The kitchen can be an intimidating place, and posting a picture of something you have made online can leave you with a comment section full of people arguing about the origin of a dish and if you can call it what you called it when it is a vegan version. Don't worry! And don't stress about cooking in a traditional way – in my opinion cookery books should not be seen as rule books. Simply think about which foods you like and what brings you joy. You can create your own version of any dish and if you don't have a particular ingredient in your cupboard, don't be quick to run out and get it. Instead, take a look at what you do have to hand, and simply replace it. You might just create a hot new dish, spark your creativity and reduce your food waste!

How to reduce food waste

HERBS AND CHILLIES

Chop fresh herbs or chillies and place them in ice cube trays to freeze them into portions. This means you have fresh herbs or chillies instead of dried if you want that extra pungent kick and the best part is that you can use them straight from the freezer – there's no need to defrost them first.

BREAD

Bread is one of the most wasted foods in the world, so do your bit to stop the waste. Slice bread and freeze it for toast, then you can simply pop it in the toaster straight from the freezer. You can also blitz stale bread in a food processor to make breadcrumbs that can be stored in a tub and frozen. See opposite for some ideas on how to use up stale bread.

'CHEESE' CLOTH

Whether you are making your own vegan cheeses, or plant-based milks (see page 23) or anything that needs straining you will eventually come across the term 'cheese cloth' (also referred to as muslin). When I started cooking I had no idea what this was but essentially it is a cloth with a fine weave that can be used for straining foods. Don't waste your money on brand new cloths. Instead, use a clean old T-shirt (washing the shirt without detergent before using it).

STOCK

A lot of the recipes in this book call for stock. To create a stock with as little waste as possible it is worth using your vegetable peelings and off-cuts to make your own stock that can be frozen and used when required. Simply pop the frozen stock in the microwave or into a saucepan and heat until melted.
To save wasting vegetable off-cuts and peelings you can pop them in a tub and keep them in the fridge or freezer until you are ready to use them.

Common wasted foods

POTATOES
We discard 5.8 million potatoes in the uk each year.

STALE BREAD
240 million slices of bread are thrown away in the UK each year.

Potatoes are amazing but you can only eat so many in one go! For a longer-lasting spud, store in a cool dark place like a cupboard, pantry or cellar. Don't wash potatoes until you are ready to use them otherwise they might rot. You can blanch and freeze potatoes, if you have a glut: peel and slice them and submerge them in a large bowl of water so they won't go brown. Bring a large pan of water to a rolling boil and drop in the potatoes for 5 minutes. Scoop them out of the water with a slotted spoon or drain using a colander. Pat dry with a clean tea towel and freeze in an airtight bag. You can store them for up to a year like this. Par-boiled potatoes can be sliced and sautéed for a quick supper, or roasted to make Waste-less Wedges (see page 128), which can be cooked and then cooled and frozen. Make Irish Potato Cakes (see page 53) with leftover mash, and Bubble and Squeak (see page 87) with leftover roasties.

To increase the life of your bread, pre-slice and freeze your loaf, then simply pop it in the toaster when you're ready for breakfast. Try the Ribollita (see page 105) for any bread that's had its day. You can also add your stale bread to a food processor and make breadcrumbs that can be stored in a tub and frozen. You can use up your stale bread in any of the following recipes in this book: Bread Sauce (see page 36), 'Bacon' Croutons (see page 76), Rice and Bean Burgers (see page 83), Ribollita (see page 105), Crumbed Piri Piri Sweet Potato (see page 126), Pizza-Stuffed Mushrooms (see page 136), Spicy Sausage Roll (see page 146), and Fruity Bread Pudding (see page 174).

BANANAS
1.4 million edible bananas are thrown away every day in the UK.

MILK
Around 5.9 million glasses of cow's milk are poured down the sink in the UK every year.

Bananas are versatile and amazing, so be sure to make the most of them. Separate them from other fruits when you store them, to help them last longer. When they get spotty, use them in smoothies or peel them and freeze them to use in smoothies or to make instant Banana Nice Cream (see page 155). When they get really dark use them to make banana bread or muffins, my Banana Custard Tarts (see page 154) or mush them into rice pudding.

It's so easy to use up milk, especially plant-based milks, as they last longer than dairy milks. You can use plant-based milk in a smoothie (see page 48), creamy sauces (see page 76), to make a rice pudding or in cakes and bakes (see pages 148–183).

SALAD

An estimated 178 million bags of salad get wasted in the UK annually.

APPLES

A staggering 1.3 million apples are thrown away in the UK each year.

Instead of opting for a plastic bag of salad, why not buy fresh lettuce heads, grow your own cress and herbs and even regrow lettuce in water? Simply cut the lettuce roughly 2.5cm (1in) up from the root and place it root-down in a glass half-filled with water and keep it topped up. The lettuce will start to regrow within just a few days. If you're buying leafy greens and won't use a full head you can use them in smoothies, pesto-style sauces or buy them frozen. This does come with added waste because of freezer bags, but they will last much longer and reduce the likelihood of you wasting those greens.

To make apples last longer, store them in a cold, dark and well-ventilated place – make sure they aren't touching each other and that they are clean and dry. Strawberry Jam Apple Pie (see page 163) and crunchy Slaw Salads (see page 80) are just a few ways you can use up apples and save them from despair. You can also cook them and freeze them.

Kitchen essentials

In this book I've strived to reduce the amount of equipment needed, and ensured the ingredients required are readily available to all.

Equipment

LARGE POT WITH A LID
I recommend a cast-iron pot because it will give you maximum flexibility between the stove-top and cooking in the oven. However, any large pot with a lid will do for this book.

LARGE BAKING TRAY
When recipe testing I used my 30 × 40cm (12 × 16in) baking tray. I recommend a large tray that fits your oven (some larger trays only fit commercial ovens and will be useless for home cooking). Buy a good sturdy tray and it will last forever.

20CM (8IN) ROUND CAKE TIN
This tin works perfectly for the Pineapple Upside-down Cake on page 172. If you use a tin with a removable base, be sure to line it well to avoid any leakage. I use a 20cm (8in) square cake tin for the brownies in this book.

LARGE SAUCEPAN
A perfect all-rounder for soups, stocks and pasta dishes. I used a large saucepan a lot when writing this book.

CHEF'S KNIFE

A 20cm (8in) plus chef's knife is a must and will do upwards of 80 per cent of all your cutting. Buy a good one that will last if you need one, but before you head to the shops, check the knife you have and see if it can be brought back to life with some sharpening.

COLANDER

I often use tongs to transfer pasta or veg from one pot to another (this allows me to save that water and repurpose it for sauces and stocks), but a large colander is always useful when washing and prepping ingredients.

WHISK

I have owned a whole host of whisks in my life, and plenty broke as soon as they met a viscous fluid. I really recommend a high-quality stainless steel whisk that will get you through thick and thin (pun intended).

FOOD PROCESSOR

You can get through this book without a food processor or stand mixer but they do make your life easier. I recommend taking a look at pre-loved equipment being sold online.

GRIDDLE PAN (RIBBED SKILLET) OR FRYING PAN

When testing the recipes in this book I used a griddle pan (ribbed skillet) for toasting bread and tortillas. I love the texture and lines that the ribs create. However, it is not essential. You can use a large frying pan or toaster instead.

Amazing Ingredients

I have heard it a million times: 'I'd love to go vegan but I couldn't give up XYZ'. It's such a common phrase. When you start off on your vegan journey you'll start to notice hints of those flavours of meat, dairy or eggs that you thought you'd miss forever in vegan dishes: you might be surprised, however, that you can replicate the textures and flavours of your favourite meat and dairy products using herbs, spices and non-animal fats.

NUTRITIONAL YEAST

This product has gained real traction over the last couple of years and can now be found on the shelves in mainstream larger supermarkets as well as health food stores. Nutritional yeast has a cheesy, nutty flavour and is perfect for adding to creamy sauces or stocks. I have used it throughout the book. What is it though? The species of yeast is known as Saccharomyces cerevisiae; it is the same yeast used for baking and brewing, but for use in savoury cooking it is sold in a flaked form and has been deactivated, meaning that it won't cause anything to rise.

ACKEE

This wonderful fruit is a complete game-changer when it comes to making vegan 'egg' dishes. Ackee is a fruit most commonly harvested in Jamaica and it is from the same family as the lychee. There is a song about the harvest of ackee that suggests picking a romantic partner that smiles, as a non-smiling partner may kill you. This refers to the fact that if ackee is picked before it is ripe and its shell has not naturally opened, then it is dangerous to eat. When cooked with kala namak (see below) it is an amazing ingredient for replicating scrambled eggs (see page 51).

KALA NAMAK

This is also known as black salt. It has a pungent sulphur smell that when added to ackee or tofu can help to replicate the taste and smell of eggs. This ingredient isn't widely available so I usually buy it online. For this reason, I have labelled it as 'optional' in this book but if you do get your hands on some it is worth it for vegan cooking. Use sparingly.

TAPIOCA FLOUR

This is the secret ingredient in a whole host of stretchy, stringy vegan cheeses. Tapioca flour has elastic properties and when added to nuts and some other ingredients can create a cheesy mozzarella-type consistency. This flour is readily available and produces such wonderful results.

AQUAFABA

It might come as a surprise to you that you may well have been pouring one of my 'amazing ingredients' down the sink your whole life. Aquafaba is the name for what is essentially chickpea juice. It is the liquid from a tin of chickpeas. When whipped, it forms a beautiful meringue consistency and can be used to create meringues, biscuits (see page 181) and batters. Don't throw it away! It will last for 2–3 days when refrigerated in a sealed jar, and can be frozen for up to 3 months, too.

YOUNG JACKFRUIT

I specify young because older jackfruit tends to be sweeter and is consumed as most other fruits. However, when jackfruit is young, and less sweet, its amazing meaty fibrous texture allows it to be marinated, cooked and used to replicate pulled pork dishes.

Pantry Essentials

Pantry essentials are going to vary depending on your taste and your go-to meals, however here is a list of some of my pantry essentials that I feel a little lost without. They also help to create lower-waste meals because they're mainly long-lasting in nature.

TINNED TOMATOES

If you have a tin of tomatoes in your cupboard then you have a world of culinary possibilities, from soups, stews and curries to pasta sauces. The best meals in life contain a tin of tomatoes. I highly recommend having a couple of tins of whole peeled plum tomatoes in your cupboard to help you create magic when the shops are shut.

DRIED PASTA

You will be able to tell from my books, and my social media, that I am a huge fan of Italian cuisine and dried pasta is an absolute must-have. Spaghetti is standard, but I usually also have orecchiette, ditaloni rigati, tagliatelle and lasagne sheets. A little tip is to use tagliatelle balls to turn your dish into a one-pot meal: simply add some extra stock to a sauce and drop in balls of tagliatelle. The pasta will soak up the flavour of the sauce, giving you a delicious dish.

DRIED BEANS AND PULSES

This will vary depending on your favourite beans. There is no need to soak your beans for hours and hours. Instead, use a quick-soak method. Add the beans to a pan and cover with water, bring to the boil and cook for 2 minutes. Allow the water to cool, cover with a lid and leave the beans to soak for 1 hour, then drain and they're good to use. This isn't as quick as opening a tin, I admit, but using dried beans and pulses will save you money and save waste as well. My favourite beans and pulses to keep handy are: pinto beans for making my own Refried Beans (see page 94); haricot beans for creating spicy Spanish Beans on Toast (see page 52); and dried lentils for creating magical Dal (see page 102).

QUINOA

As a vegan, quinoa is a must to have around. It is a high protein, high amino acid 'super food' that is great to add to salads, soups and even cakes. Cook a big batch, pop it in a tub and keep it in the fridge for up to 1 week; that way you always have some to add to your dishes without the added labour of cooking it.

BAKING BASICS

Flour, caster sugar, baking powder, yeast and salt. Now, have I cheated by adding multiple ingredients to one section? Undoubtedly so, but these make up my baking basics. If you have these ingredients in your cupboards you can create a whole host of wonderful baked goods and desserts.

STOCK CUBES

Stock cubes are great to have handy if you haven't prepared any fresh stock. I use stock prepared ahead of time and frozen, or liquid seasoning, to give my dishes that flavour hit. Liquid seasonings can be called a whole host of things such as 'liquid aminos' or 'brownings', and they add a great flavour to noodles, broths, gravies and ragus.

SWEET JARRED ROASTED RED PEPPERS

These are a real treat. They are perfect for creating rich, decadent sauces or adding to your pasta or pizza.

PLANT-BASED MILK

Milk is much more than just something to add to your tea or coffee. Vegan milks are versatile – go to your nearest store, buy a few types and try them out; you will quickly recognise the strengths and weaknesses of each milk, and which you prefer the taste of. Cashew milk is one of my favourites because of its incredibly rich creamy texture; hemp milk has fantastic nutritional benefits (it has a rather earthy taste, making it ideal for flavoured protein shakes); and oat and soy milks are good all-rounders (check out my milk recipe on page 34). Any vegan milk labelled 'barista' is great for your hot drinks.

DARK CHOCOLATE

It might seem strange to include this as a pantry essential but the truth is I just love it! Vegan dark chocolate is perfect for having to hand, especially during your transition to veganism. Dark chocolate will give you that sweet hit for when you are craving dessert and may not have anything vegan to hand. It is also great to know you have it at home if the restaurant your family or friends picked didn't have a vegan dessert. I like to add it to spicy savoury dishes like chilli, too. It's definitely worth giving it a go!

Freezer Essentials

VEGAN ICE CREAM

There are so many vegan ice cream options out there, and they last for months. Unfortunately, not every restaurant has vegan options on the menu. That is why I advise keeping a tub of your favourite in the freezer so you don't go home from a meal out disappointed.

LEAFY GREENS

Bagged salad and leafy greens are thrown away in huge amounts. Instead of risking wasting these amazing greens, remove the stalks, roughly chop the leaves and keep them in a bag or tub in the freezer. You can pop them into stews, curries and ragus to add extra nourishment whenever you need them. This also works with spinach, kale, cavolo nero and all cabbage greens.

BANANAS

When bananas are nice and ripe but you know you have too many to use up they are perfect to peel, pop in a tub and freeze. Bananas will keep for months in the freezer and can be used in a whole host of recipes. Try Banana Nice Cream (see page 155) or Green Smoothies (see page 48). You can also pair up the Peanut Butter Cookies (see page 152) and banana nice cream to make an ice-cream sandwich.

PEAS

Give them a chance! Peas are one of my most used ingredients, mainly because they go in just about anything and are full of protein and just half a cup gives you 34 per cent of your RDI of vitamin A. You can chuck them straight in your stews or ragus from frozen and just simmer them for 5 minutes to defrost. Try blending them with pesto and stock to create a beautiful pesto and pea soup.

FROZEN FRUIT AND BERRIES

Cherries, blueberries, mango, raspberries and many more are widely available in supermarkets. They are amazing to have handy for a morning smoothie, making a fruit crumble no matter the season or to make a compote. Fresh berries are great too but their shelf-life often leads to waste – and berries are too good to waste.

CHILLIES

I love spice, but I rarely get through a whole bag of red chillies in one go. Don't let them go to waste. Instead, pop them in a freezer bag and bring them out when you need them. You can chop them up from frozen or – better still – just grate them into the dish from frozen.

PANTRY RECIPES

Hummus
Vegetable stock
Vegetable gravy
Oat milk
Bread sauce
Cheesy mustard sauce
Zero-waste pesto
Vegan cheese
Parmesan-style topping
Vegan 'meat' (chickn') seasoning

Making your own hummus is almost a rite of passage for budding vegan cooks. Basic hummus consists of chickpeas, tahini, garlic and olive oil. But adding your own upgrades is a must to discover your ultimate vegan hummus. Try roasting your own sweet red peppers or get the jarred version if you are in a rush.

This is perfect served with freshly toasted flatbreads.

Hummus

SERVES 6 AS A DIP

1 × 400g (14oz) tin chickpeas, drained and rinsed
juice of 1 large lemon
60ml (¼ cup) tahini
2 garlic cloves, crushed
50g (1¾oz) roasted red peppers (optional)
50ml (scant ¼ cup) extra virgin olive oil, plus extra to serve
Sea salt
Pinch of smoked paprika, to serve

Put all the ingredients, except the smoked paprika, in a food processor and blitz until smooth, adding a splash of water to loosen it if necessary. Transfer to a serving dish, drizzle with extra olive oil and dust with the smoked paprika.

The hummus will keep well in the fridge, in an airtight container, for up to 1 week.

Vegetable stock is nutritious and very simple to make, and using homemade stock makes such a difference to dishes such as bolognese, risottos, stews and soups. It is the foundation of a great homemade gravy, can be created using leftovers and is a great waste-reducing tool.

The ingredients listed below are just for guidance: feel free to use vegetable offcuts and even peelings. Remember to always wash your vegetables before chopping and peeling, to help make a clean and tasty stock.

Vegetable stock

MAKES 1 LITRE (4 CUPS)

1–2 onions
2–3 carrots
3–4 celery sticks
4–5 sprigs of thyme
1 bay leaf
2 tsp finely chopped fresh or dried thyme
Small bunch of parsley
1 tsp black peppercorns
Optional extras: leeks, fennel, tomatoes, mushrooms, mushroom stems, parsnips

Put all the ingredients in a large saucepan, cover with 1.5 litres (6½ cups) of cold water. Bring to a simmer and cook gently for around 1 hour.

If you are using the stock straight away, very carefully strain the liquid through a sieve. If you are making stock in advance, leave it to cool, then store in an airtight container and keep in the fridge for up to 2 weeks, or in the freezer for up to 3 months.

There are plenty of vegetable gravies on the market, but making your own has a host of advantages when it comes to creating next-level dishes. For one, you can tailor your gravy to suit the dish you're making: try adding a teaspoon of mustard or BBQ sauce to mix up your vegan bangers and mash for example.

Vegetable gravy

MAKES 700ML (3 CUPS)

60ml (¼ cup) olive oil
1 medium onion, finely diced
2 garlic cloves, crushed
4 tbsp plain flour
250ml (1 cup) oat milk (shop-bought or see recipe on page 34)
1 tsp Marmite
500ml (2 cups) vegan vegetable stock (cube/powdered, or see recipe on page 31)
½ tsp ground black pepper
Sea salt

Heat the olive oil in a saucepan over a medium heat, then add the onion and garlic and fry for a few minutes until very soft and translucent.

Mix the flour and a little of the milk together in a cup or bowl to form a paste, then add the rest of the milk to the paste and whisk it in so that the flour and milk are well combined and free of lumps.

Add the flour and milk mix to the saucepan along with the Marmite and vegetable stock and whisk to combine. Bring to the boil, whisking constantly, then let it boil for a few minutes until it thickens to make a thick but pourable gravy. Add the black pepper and some sea salt to taste.

When I was first learning to make vegan milks and cheeses, the term 'cheese cloth' came up a lot. Take it from me, it isn't worth seeking out. Simply use a clean old T-shirt (soaking it in water and re-drying it to get rid of any detergent first) and save yourself time, money and trouble. You may want to alter the water quantity, depending how creamy or thin you want your milk: the amount below makes a creamy milk.

Have a play with the recipe to get your coffee, tea or breakfast the way you like it. Oh, and try adding cocoa powder when blending. Because no one can make you grow up, right?

Oat milk

MAKES 1 LITRE (4 CUPS)

90g (1 cup) rolled oats
Pinch of sea salt
1 tbsp maple syrup or
    golden syrup
½ tsp vanilla extract
    (optional)

Put the oats, salt, syrup and vanilla extract (if using) in a high-speed blender with 1 litre (4 cups) water. Put the lid on and blend for 30–60 seconds, or until the mixture seems well combined. It doesn't need to be completely smooth.

Cover a large mixing bowl or jug with a very thin towel or a clean T-shirt. Pour in the blended mixture, then lift the shirt from the sides and squeeze the milk through the towel or T-shirt into your bowl.

Transfer to an airtight container and chill. The milk will keep in the fridge for up to 5 days.

Bread sauce is a thick, gooey, delicious way to save old, unloved bread from the bin. Give it a go for your Sunday dinner. Roast potatoes and bread sauce are a match made in heaven after all.

Bread sauce

SERVES 4 AS A SAUCE

50g (1¾oz) vegan butter
1 small onion, finely diced
¼ tsp ground cloves
Pinch of ground nutmeg
½ tsp sea salt
1 tsp freshly ground black pepper
120g (2 cups) breadcrumbs (made from stale bread)
600ml (2½ cups) oat milk (shop-bought or see recipe on page 34)

Melt the butter in a saucepan over a medium heat and add the onion. Sauté for a few minutes until translucent then stir in the cloves, nutmeg, salt and pepper. Add the breadcrumbs then cover with the oat milk. Stir continuously as it bubbles and let it cook for about 20 minutes, until thickened. Remove from the heat.

This sauce is a really simple recipe that will add a decadent wow factor to any of your roast dinners or pastry dishes.

Cheesy mustard sauce

MAKES 300ML (1¼ CUPS) – ENOUGH FOR 4 AS A SAUCE

1 tsp Dijon mustard
3 tbsp nutritional yeast
300ml (1¼ cups) plant-based milk (oat or cashew work great)
100g (3½oz) vegan cheese, grated

Put the mustard in a small saucepan over a low heat. Sprinkle in the nutritional yeast and stir together to create a paste. Gradually pour in the milk, whisking as it starts to warm up. Once it starts to bubble, add the grated cheese and gently whisk it in until melted and combined. Remove from the heat and serve straight away.

Bagged salad is one of the most wasted food items in Britain, so finding creative ways to use it is important. Zero-waste pesto is the perfect way to use up your old salad leaves. This recipe is totally flexible, to help you make the most of what is in your cupboards. You can stick to the classic route and use pine nuts and basil, or you can go rogue with Brazil nuts or cashews. You might just find a new favourite sauce.

Serve with cooked pasta, as a salad dressing or as a dip for bread or chips.

Zero-waste pesto

MAKES ENOUGH FOR 6 SERVINGS OF PASTA

100g (⅔ cup) any nuts (pine nuts are traditional, yet Brazil nuts and cashews work amazingly, too)
¼ tsp sea salt
3 garlic cloves
3 tbsp nutritional yeast
70g leftover bagged salad
50g fresh basil
4 tbsp olive oil
Juice of ½ lemon

Put the nuts in a food processor with the salt, garlic and nutritional yeast and blitz until the mixture forms crumbs (this can also be done in a pestle and mortar). Add the leaves, basil, olive oil and lemon juice and pulse a few times until the pesto has a finely chopped consistency. Transfer to a container.

The pesto will keep in the fridge, in an airtight container, for up to 1 week.

Mozzarella is the ultimate pizza cheese, and making pizza is amazing, but balls of plant-based mozzarella for tearing and adding on top (either before or after baking) turn it into a real vegan treat!

Vegan cheese

MAKES 4 MOZZARELLA-STYLE BALLS

100g (⅔ cup) cashews, soaked overnight, then drained and rinsed

200ml (generous ¾ cup) cold water

1 tbsp nutritional yeast

2 tsp apple cider vinegar

1 tsp sea salt

¼ tsp garlic powder

3 tbsp tapioca flour

Put all the ingredients in a high-speed blender or food processor and blend until smooth.

Transfer the mixture to a saucepan, place over a low heat and cook, stirring, as it starts to thicken. After about 5 minutes it will come together into a ball like a wet dough. Remove from the heat.

Get your hands wet, then grab chunks of the warm vegan cheese, roll into mozzarella-sized (golf ball-sized) balls, and drop into a bowl of cold water to set (they should set within 30 seconds).

Chill in the fridge for 1 hour before using. They will keep in an airtight container, in the fridge, with a drizzle of oil for up to 5 days.

This isn't the style of hard cheese you would traditionally add to pasta dishes like carbonara, but it's a satisfying alternative to a little sprinkle of Parmesan on pasta and salad dishes.

Parmesan-style topping

MAKES 230G (8OZ)

25g (1oz) fine
   breadcrumbs
25g (1oz) nutritional
   yeast
60g (½ cup) grated
   vegan hard/firm
   cheese
120g (1 cup) Brazil nuts
1 tsp garlic granules

Put all the ingredients in a food processor and blitz to a fine crumb. Transfer to an airtight container and store in the fridge for up to 1 month.

When people imagine a roast chicken dinner they think of all of the aromas and flavours... SURPRISE! These can be created using plants. Give this Chickn' seasoning a go and transform your tofu, seitan, mushrooms or soy into a tasty chicken-flavoured dish.

Vegan 'meat' (chickn') seasoning

MAKES 40G (1½OZ)

Grated zest of 1 lemon
1 tbsp dried thyme
1 tbsp garlic granules
1 tbsp dried parsley
½ tbsp dried tarragon
1 tsp turmeric
1 tsp freshly ground
   black pepper
1 tsp sea salt
Pinch of sugar

Combine all the ingredients in a jar and leave loosely covered for 24 hours, then seal. The mixture will keep well in an airtight container for up to 1 month.

BREAKFAST

Green smoothie
Iced banana smoothie
Ackee eggs
Spanish beans on toast
Irish potato cakes
Granola
Blueberry breakfast muffins
French toast nachos
Breakfast squares

The ultimate waste-saving meal is of course the smoothie. You can pop whatever you have in the blender and mix it up. Try adding leafy greens to your smoothie.

Green smoothie

SERVES 2

300ml (1¼ cups) plant-
   based milk
1 frozen banana
½ cucumber
60g (2oz) greens
   (whatever is going to
   waste, such as kale or
   bagged salad, work
   perfectly)
100g (3½oz) frozen fruit
   (I like to use mango if
   I want it to be a green
   smoothie)
1 tsp turmeric
1 tsp ground flaxseed
Agave or maple syrup,
   to taste (optional)

Put the milk in a blender, then add all of the other ingredients and blend until smooth. Feel free to sweeten to taste with agave or maple syrup.

This is a great morning drink to kickstart your day. It has everything you need to wake you up, reduce those morning aches and satisfy those hunger cravings first thing. It is also quick and easy.

Iced banana latte

SERVES 2

100ml (scant ½ cup) shot of coffee made with 2 tsp instant espresso powder
1 ripe banana
½ tsp ground cinnamon, plus extra to serve (optional)
½ tsp ground nutmeg
1 tsp ground turmeric
1 tsp freshly ground black pepper
1 tsp vanilla extract
Ice cubes
200ml (generous ¾ cup) cold plant-based milk

Simply put all of the ingredients in a blender and blend until smooth. Divide between 2 cups and sprinkle with a pinch of ground cinnamon, if using.

Full disclosure, this recipe is incredibly simple. Tinned ackee can be a little pricey but I urge you to give it a go. This incredible fruit is used in traditional Caribbean recipes and creates wonderful vegan 'scrambled egg'. Try serving it with spinach and cherry tomatoes.

Ackee eggs

SERVES 2

Olive oil, for frying
2 garlic cloves, finely chopped
1 tsp dried oregano
2 tbsp nutritional yeast
½ tsp kala namak/ Himalayan black salt (optional – use regular sea salt if you can't source it)
1 × 540g (19oz) tin ackee
Freshly ground black pepper, to taste
2 slices of sourdough (or any bread you have), toasted

Heat 1 teaspoon olive oil in a frying pan over a low heat, add the garlic and sauté for a few minutes until softened, then add the oregano, nutritional yeast and kala namak (if using) and stir.

Open the tin of ackee and carefully drain away the excess liquid. Tip the delicate ackee into the pan and very gently stir to combine it with the oregano. Keep the pan over a medium-low heat until the ackee has broken up slightly and is warmed through. Remove from the heat and serve on sourdough toast and a grinding of black pepper.

Beans on toast is a classic dish enjoyed by all. And it's easy to make your own variation, ditching the familiar tinned version (and the nasty preservatives, too) for a more wholesome and even tastier dish.

Spanish beans on toast

SERVES 2

Olive oil, for frying
4 garlic cloves, finely
   chopped
50g (½ cup) sundried
   tomatoes in oil,
   drained and roughly
   chopped
½ tsp chilli flakes
1 tsp smoked paprika
100g (½ cup) beans
   (haricot or cannellini),
   quick-soaked (see
   page 22) or use
   150g/5½oz tinned,
   drained and rinsed
125ml (½ cup) passata
5g fresh parsley, finely
   chopped, or 1 tsp
   dried parsley
2 slices of toast
Organic avocado or
   Pesto (see page 38),
   to serve (optional)

Heat a drizzle of olive oil in a saucepan over a medium heat and add the garlic, sundried tomatoes and chilli flakes. Sauté for a few minutes until the garlic is softened, then add the smoked paprika, beans and passata. Stir and simmer for 5–10 minutes until it reaches your desired thickness.

Add to your toast and serve garnished with parsley and your choice of topping: I recommend organic avocado, or a teaspoon of pesto (for a lower environmental-impact option).

Irish potato cakes have always been the style of potato cakes I make, purely because they're delicious and simple. Mashed potatoes are sticky and don't need anything to bind them. These have a rugged hearty feel and that's what I love!

I like to serve these with beans and vegan sausages for a hearty breakfast. But they go with anything; try them with any soup, stew, curry or dhal.

Irish potato cakes

SERVES 2

400g (14oz) mashed
    potato
100g (scant 1 cup) plain
    flour, plus extra for
    dusting
1 tsp baking powder
1 tsp salt

Mix all of the ingredients together in a mixing bowl until they form a ball. Tip the ball onto a floured surface and divide it in half, then flatten each into a disc shape roughly 1cm (½in) thick and the size of your frying pan. Now cut each disc into quarters, so you have 8 pieces.

Put a dry frying pan over a medium heat, pop 4 pieces in the pan and cook for 10 minutes, carefully flipping them halfway through. As there's no oil in the pan the potato cakes won't become golden brown when cooked – they will have more of a wet sand colour. You're looking for a firm, rugged potato cake. Transfer the 4 cakes to a warm plate and cook the remaining 4 cakes.

Remove from the heat and serve.

Granola is a sweet, savoury, delicious breakfast treat that keeps for a very long time when stored correctly. It is made using dried ingredients and keeps dry and fresh so it is a perfect recipe for the low-waste chef who wants to enjoy the luxuries of granola.

Granola

MAKES ENOUGH FOR 6 SERVINGS

2 tbsp vegetable oil
150ml (⅔ cup) maple or golden syrup
3 tsp vanilla extract
300g (3 cups) rolled oats
50g (scant ⅓ cup) pumpkin seeds
100g (generous 1 cup) flaked almonds
100g (⅔ cup) dried apricots (or pitted chopped dates or raisins)

Preheat the oven to 170°C/150°C Fan/325°F/gas 3 and line two baking sheets with greaseproof paper.

Combine the oil, syrup and vanilla extract in a large bowl. Tip in all the remaining ingredients, except the dried fruit, and mix well.

Tip the granola onto the lined baking sheets and spread it out evenly. Bake in the oven for 15 minutes, then scatter over the dried fruit, stir the mixture with a wooden spoon and bake for a further 10–15 minutes until lightly golden brown. Remove and transfer the granola to a flat tray to cool. Serve with cold plant-based milk.

The granola will keep in an airtight container for up to 1 month.

Breakfast can be a wonderful experience, filled with decadent dishes galore, but when you are late for work and have to decide between showering or brushing your teeth, a pre-made muffin to eat on the go is a lifesaver.

Blueberry breakfast muffins

MAKES 8 MUFFINS

140g (1 cup) blueberries (fresh or frozen)

DRY INGREDIENTS
160g (1⅓ cups) plain flour
50g (¼ cup) quinoa
2 tbsp chia seeds
50g (¼ cup) caster sugar
2 tsp baking powder
½ tsp sea salt

WET INGREDIENTS
250ml (1 cup) oat milk (shop-bought or see recipe on page 34)
60ml (¼ cup) vegetable oil
1 tbsp lemon juice
2 tsp vanilla extract

Preheat the oven to 200°C/180°C Fan/400°F/gas 6 and line a 12-hole muffin tin with 8 muffin cases.

Put the dry ingredients in a large bowl and rub everything through your fingers, as if making pastry, to ensure the ingredients are evenly blended.

Mix the wet ingredients in a jug, then pour into the bowl of dry ingredients and fold together.

Fold the blueberries into the batter and divide evenly among the 8 muffin cases, filling the cases to the brim. Bake for 30 minutes until risen and golden. Remove from the oven and either serve warm or cold.

The muffins will keep in an airtight container for up to 5 days.

I love French toast and I love nachos, so this was a no-brainer. For me, these sit right alongside pancakes as a decadent breakfast item. Try them drizzled with maple syrup or even melted chocolate.

French toast nachos

SERVES 2

4 tortillas
1 tbsp vegetable oil
4 tbsp ground flaxseed
1 tsp vanilla extract
180ml (¾ cup) oat milk (or other plant-based milk)
A drizzle of maple syrup, to serve

FOR DUSTING
1 tbsp icing sugar
2 tsp ground cinnamon

Preheat the oven to 180°C/160°C Fan/350°F/gas 4 and line a large baking tray with greaseproof paper.

Stack the tortillas on top of each other and carefully cut them into 8 triangles (to make 32 triangles in total). Put the vegetable oil, flaxseed, vanilla extract and oat milk in a bowl and whisk to combine and form a batter.

Dip the small triangles into the batter to coat them in the mixture, then remove them one by one and lay them on the lined baking tray, trying to space them out as much as possible.

Bake in the oven for 20 minutes, until they go golden brown and crispy.

While they are in the oven, combine the icing sugar and cinnamon in a bowl. Remove the French toast nachos from the oven and dust with the icing sugar and cinnamon mixture.

Serve with a drizzle of maple syrup.

These crunchy squares fall somewhere between a flapjack and a breakfast bar; tasty squares of granola goodness, perfect to take with you on the go.

Breakfast squares

MAKE 9 BARS

100g (1 cup) almonds (or nut of your choice)
1 tsp vegetable oil
220g (1 cup) dates
135g (1½ cups) rolled oats
60ml (¼ cup) golden syrup
60g (¼ cup) creamy salted natural peanut butter or almond butter
200g (7oz) vegan dark chocolate chips or broken dark chocolate
100g (¾ cup) raisins or chopped apricots

Preheat the oven to 180°C/160°C Fan/350°F/gas 4 and line a 20cm (8in) square baking tin with greaseproof paper.

Put the almonds in a large bowl, add the vegetable oil and coat the nuts in the oil. Tip the nuts onto a baking tray, spread them out and toast in the oven for 5 minutes. Remove and shake gently, then return to the oven for a further 5 minutes.

Blend the dates in a high-speed blender until they form a smooth paste. Place the oats, roasted almonds and blitzed dates in a large bowl.

Warm the syrup and nut butter in a small saucepan over a low heat until smooth, then mix the warm ingredients into the oats, almonds, dates and chocolate until combined. Press the mixture into the lined tin.

Cover the tin with a tea towel and place in the fridge for at least an hour to firm up.

Cut into 9 bars to enjoy on the go. They will keep, stored in an airtight container in the fridge, for up to 2 weeks.

LUNCH

64

Cauliflower soup
Sweet pepper and tomato soup
Spicy pineapple salad
Quesadillas three ways
Pizzadilla | BBQ jackfruit | Veggie supreme
Charred romaine salad
Lemon and cashew spaghetti
Spaghetti Napolitano
Slaw salad
Rice and bean burgers
Rice and beans
Baked garlic
Bubble and squeak
Leek and spinach pie
Puttanesca tart
Garlic mushroom tart
Refried beans
Chuna pasta

When cooking with cauliflower I love using up all of the awesome little florets, but the stalks and leaves can often end up getting left out. This recipe shows those stalks and leaves some love! If there is half a cauliflower in your fridge that's been forgotten about, go grab it now.

Cauliflower soup

SERVES 4

Drizzle of olive oil
5 garlic cloves, chopped
1 red onion, roughly
   chopped
1 leek, thinly sliced
1 cauliflower with
   leaves, florets,
   trimmed stalk and
   leaves chopped into
   small pieces
Handful of cashews
   (optional)
5 tbsp nutritional yeast
2 tsp sea salt
3 tsp freshly ground
   black pepper
2 tsp smoked paprika

TO SERVE
200g (7oz) cooked
   cavolo nero, or frozen
   spinach (defrosted
   and heated through)
Crusty bread

Heat the olive oil in a saucepan over a low heat, add the chopped garlic, onion and leek and fry for 5 minutes, then add the cauliflower and leaves (add cashews if using). Cook for a further 10 minutes, then add the nutritional yeast, salt, pepper and paprika and stir to coat all of the ingredients in the seasoning. Add 1 litre (4 cups) of boiling water, stir and simmer for 30 minutes.

Use a slotted spoon to scoop out the chunky bits (cauliflower and onion) and add them to the blender. Add a little of the soup from the pan and blend until smooth. Add the blended mixture back to the pan with the rest of the soup and stir to combine.

Serve with cavolo nero and crusty bread.

This is one of my all-time favourite soups. There's nothing better than a sweet pepper and tomato soup with a large chunk of crusty bread.

Sweet pepper and tomato soup

SERVES 4

Extra virgin olive oil
8 medium tomatoes, quartered
1 small onion, cut into 6 pieces
2 red peppers, deseeded and quartered
6 garlic cloves, unpeeled
1.25 litres (5 cups) vegan vegetable stock (made from a cube/powder, or see recipe on page 31)
½ tsp cayenne
¼ tsp smoked paprika
90g (½ cup) cooked quinoa
Sea salt and freshly ground black pepper

Preheat the oven to 190°C/170°C Fan/375°F/gas 5 and place two racks in the middle of the oven.

Brush two baking trays lightly with olive oil. Place the tomatoes, skin side down, on one of them.

Gently toss the onion and red peppers lightly with olive oil. Place on the other baking tray, with the red peppers skin side down. Place the unpeeled garlic cloves on the tray, too.

Place both trays in the oven for 35–45 minutes, until the vegetables are tender throughout and turning golden on the edges.

Bring the stock to the boil in a large saucepan over a medium-high heat. Peel the roasted garlic and toss it in. Add the roasted tomatoes, peppers and onion, cayenne and smoked paprika. Simmer for 10 minutes, reducing the heat as necessary to maintain a steady simmer.

Purée the soup using an immersion blender or transfer the soup to a blender, a few cups at a time, and blend until smooth. Season to taste with salt and pepper. Add the cooked quinoa and stir.

This spicy pineapple salad is a tasty, refreshing and filling salad that pairs perfectly with vegan mayo or yoghurt. Feel free to adjust the spice as you like it.

Spiced pineapple salad

SERVES 2

1 medium pineapple, peeled
2 tsp smoked paprika
Pinch of sea salt
1 corn cob, kernels cut from core (or 165g/6oz tinned corn)
2 romaine lettuce heads (or other lettuce)
1 fresh red chilli, finely chopped

Heat a griddle pan (ribbed skillet) over a high heat.

Cut the pineapple fruit away from the core in long rectangle chunks and place them on a plate or tray.

Sprinkle the paprika and salt onto the pineapple and massage it all over before placing the chunks onto the hot pan. Griddle for a few minutes on each side, until charred. Sprinkle the corn into the pan and allow to slightly char. They will start to catch and darken on the outer edges.

Roughly chop the heads of romaine lettuce and divide between two large bowls. Sprinkle over the finely chopped chilli and griddled corn, then place the charred pineapple on top.

Serve with sweet chilli sauce or my creamy salad sauce (see page 76).

Quesadilla three ways

Quesadillas make a simple, quick, delicious lunch that is fully customisable. Here are three recipes to get you started, then take it from there and create quesadilla magic. I want to see all of your weird and wonderful combinations.

A few suggested toppings are:
Avocado
Vegan mayonnaise or soured cream
Hot Sauce
Vegetables of choice

Pizzadilla

SERVES 4

8 tortillas
240ml (1 cup) passata
(4 tbsp for each
quesadilla)
180g (6½oz) vegan
cheese, grated
2 tsp dried chilli flakes
5 tbsp jarred artichokes,
drained and chopped
10 pitted olives, cut into
rings
2 garlic cloves, finely
chopped
4 tsp dried oregano

Preheat the oven to 200°C/180°C Fan/400°F/gas 6.

Lay four of the tortillas out on a board. Spread 2 tablespoons of passata on each tortilla like sauce on a pizza. Scatter on half the grated vegan cheese followed by all the other ingredients, except the oregano, and pop the remaining tortillas on top.

Place the sandwiched tortillas on a baking tray and top with the remaining passata (2 tablespoons per quesadilla), the remaining vegan cheese and the oregano. You could also use an ovenproof frying pan, but you'd need to cook them one at a time.

Bake in the oven for 8 minutes until they are toasted and the cheese has melted, remove from the oven, slice into quarters and eat warm.

BBQ jackfruit

SERVES 4

8 tortillas
8 tbsp passata
4 tbsp BBQ sauce
200g (7oz) vegan
  cheese, grated
1 × 400g (14oz) tin
  young jackfruit,
  drained and broken up
  with a fork (250g/9oz
  drained weight)
½ onion, roughly
  chopped
2 garlic cloves, finely
  chopped
Handful of spinach,
  finely chopped
Pinch of sea salt

Lay four of the tortillas out on a board. Mix the passata with the BBQ sauce, then spread it on the four tortillas like sauce on a pizza. Scatter on your grated vegan cheese, top with all the other ingredients and top with the remaining four tortillas.

Place a large frying pan over a low heat. Carefully place a quesadilla in the pan and cook gently for a few minutes, until it is lightly browned on the bottom, then flip it over by laying a small plate on top and using this to turn the quesadilla out of the pan, then slide it back in on the uncooked side. Cook for a further 3–4 minutes. Repeat with the remaining tortillas.

Veggie supreme

SERVES 4

8 tortillas

4 tbsp passata

180g (6½oz) vegan cheese, grated

½ onion, roughly chopped

2 garlic cloves, finely chopped

Handful of spinach, finely chopped

2 red peppers, deseeded and thinly sliced

100g (2 cups) chestnut mushrooms, thinly sliced

Lay four of the tortillas out on a board. Spread the passata on the four tortillas like sauce on a pizza. Scatter on your grated vegan cheese, top with all the other ingredients and top with the remaining four tortillas.

Place a large frying pan over a low heat. Carefully place a quesadilla in the pan and cook gently for a few minutes, until lightly browned on the bottom, then flip it over by laying a small plate on top and using this to turn the quesadilla out of the pan then slide it back in on the uncooked side. Cook for a further 3–4 minutes. Repeat with the remaining tortillas.

This warm and satisfying romaine salad, with a creamy salad sauce and crunchy 'bacon' croutons (a tasty way to use up stale bread), is a great alternative to a Caesar salad.

Charred romaine salad

SERVES 4

FOR THE 'BACON' CROUTONS
100g (3½oz) bread, cubed
3 tbsp olive oil
1 tsp smoked paprika
1 tbsp crushed garlic
½ tsp soy sauce
1 tsp dried oregano
1 tbsp nutritional yeast

FOR THE SALAD
2 large heads of romaine lettuce, halved lengthways
2 firm, ripe tomatoes, cut into small cubes (or 10 cherry tomatoes, halved)
60g (½ cup) defrosted frozen peas

FOR THE CREAMY SALAD SAUCE
75g cashews, soaked overnight, then drained and rinsed
150ml (⅔ cup) plant-based milk
1 tsp Dijon mustard
2 tbsp nutritional yeast

Preheat the oven to 180°C/160°C Fan/350°F/gas 4 and line a baking tray with greaseproof paper.

Place the cubed bread in a bowl. Mix the oil, smoked paprika, garlic, soy sauce, oregano and nutritional yeast together and pour the mixture over the bread. Massage the mixture into the bread cubes then tip them onto the lined baking tray and bake for 15 minutes until crisp.

Heat a griddle pan (ribbed skillet) over a high heat. Place the romaine lettuce halves cut side down on the griddle pan and char for a few minutes each.

To make the creamy salad sauce, put the soaked cashews, milk, mustard and nutritional yeast in a blender and blend until smooth.

Place the grilled romaine on plates and scatter with the tomato, peas and croutons. Pour over the rich, creamy sauce to serve.

This lemon and cashew spaghetti recipe is a 15-minute meal that feels like a 5-star dish. It is simplicity in all its glory.

Lemon and cashew spaghetti

SERVES 2

100g (3½oz) spaghetti
2 tbsp olive oil
1 fresh red chilli,
    deseeded and finely
    chopped
2 garlic cloves, finely
    diced
1 tbsp nutritional yeast
20g (¼ cup) cashew
    flour (cashews blitzed
    to a fine crumb)
Grated zest of 1 lemon
    and juice of ½
Handful of fresh or
    frozen block spinach
Pinch of sea salt

TO SERVE
15g (a handful) fresh
    basil leaves, chopped
Cracked black pepper

Cook the spaghetti in a large saucepan of salted boiling water, following the packet instructions.

Heat the olive oil in a frying pan over a medium heat. Add the chilli and garlic and cook for a few minutes, then add the nutritional yeast, cashew flour, lemon zest and spinach and stir together. Add 60ml (¼ cup) of the pasta cooking water and juice of half the lemon.

As soon as the pasta is al dente use a pair of tongs to take it straight from the water and into the frying pan. Toss in the sauce until coated. Remove from the heat, add the salt and basil and stir, then serve scattered with cracked black pepper.

One of the most easiest spaghetti dishes, spaghetti Napolitano is easily one of my favourites. It's really simple to cook but so warming and tasty to eat.

Spaghetti Napolitano

SERVES 2

100g (3½oz) spaghetti
50g (½ cup) sundried tomatoes in oil, roughly chopped (plus some oil from the jar)
2 garlic cloves, finely chopped
8 cherry tomatoes, quartered
120ml (½ cup) passata
Pinch of sea salt
1 tsp cracked black pepper
1 tsp parsley (dried or fresh, chopped)

Cook the spaghetti in a large saucepan of salted boiling water, following the packet instructions.

Heat a drizzle of the sundried tomato oil in a frying pan over a medium heat. Add the garlic and cherry tomatoes and soften for a few minutes. Add the sundried tomatoes, passata, salt and pepper and let it simmer and thicken slightly until the pasta is ready to add.

Remove the pasta from the water with tongs and add to the frying pan. Toss in the sauce until coated.

Serve, garnished with a sprinkle of parsley.

Salads are awesome when they're done right, and this slaw salad is a tangy treat. You can add some vegan mayo to make it creamy, or apple cider vinegar to change it up.

Slaw salad

SERVES 2

100g (3½oz) trimmed
  kale
2 tbsp lemon juice
1 carrot, grated
1 medium apple, cored
  and thinly sliced
¼ white cabbage, thinly
  sliced (red cabbage
  works too)
1 small red onion, thinly
  sliced
20g (¼ cup) roughly
  chopped dried fruit
  (such as apricots,
  raisins or dried
  cherries, chopped
  dried dates)
20g (¼ cup) pumpkin
  seeds (or chopped
  nuts)
75g (⅓ cup) Zero-waste
  Pesto (see page 38) or
  vegan shop-bought
  pesto
1 courgette

Put the kale in a large bowl and pour over the lemon juice. Use your hands to massage the kale with the lemon juice for a minute or two: the citric acid in the lemon juice will 'cook' and soften the kale.

Add the carrot, apple, cabbage, red onion, dried fruit, pumpkin seeds and pesto and mix together.

Using a vegetable peeler, peel the courgette into long strips and roll them up to create a decorative element and place them on top of the slaw.

Bean burgers are awesome, but I wanted to create some that would really stand out at a BBQ, and these rice and bean burgers really do that. Try changing up the BBQ sauce for hot sauce or adding some chopped garlic for extra flavour.

If you are going to grill them, try freezing them first for an extra 'meaty' burger.

Rice and bean burgers

SERVES 6

Drizzle of olive oil
4 garlic cloves, finely chopped
1 onion, finely diced
60g (½ cup) breadcrumbs
200g (1 cup) cooked and cooled brown rice
1 × 400g (14oz) tin black beans, drained and rinsed
1 tsp dried oregano
1 tsp smoked paprika
1 tsp freshly ground black pepper
5 tbsp nutritional yeast
60ml (¼ cup) BBQ sauce
1 tsp sea salt
Burger buns, salad and favourite toppings, to serve

Heat the olive oil in a frying pan over a medium heat. Add the garlic and onion and sauté for a few minutes until soft and lightly golden.

Put the breadcrumbs in a food processor with the rice, beans and onion and garlic mixture, oregano, smoked paprika, black pepper, nutritional yeast and BBQ sauce and pulse until evenly combined (but not puréed).

Remove the mixture from the food processor and divide it evenly into 6 pieces. Roll each piece into a ball and press flat into a patty.

Sprinkle some salt on both sides of the burgers, then fry in a dry frying pan over a medium heat for 5 minutes on each side, or grill on both sides until they begin to char.

Serve in burger buns with lettuce and your favourite toppings.

My rice and beans are a great way to enjoy this amazing combination of ingredients with minimum effort required. Try adding some dark leafy greens, such as cavolo nero, when you add the rice.

Rice and beans

SERVES 6

400g (2 cups) dried red
   or pinto beans, soaked
   (overnight, or see
   quick-soak method on
   page 22), then drained
   and rinsed
Drizzle of olive oil
5 garlic cloves, finely
   chopped
2 leeks, sliced
1 onion, finely chopped
1 carrot, halved
   lengthways and
   chopped
4 fresh tomatoes, finely
   chopped
1 green pepper,
   deseeded and diced
Pinch of sea salt
1 tsp dried oregano
1 tsp ground cumin
1 tsp smoked paprika
5 tbsp nutritional yeast
3 fresh chillies, or to
   taste, finely chopped
200g (1 cup) basmati
   rice

Put the beans in a large saucepan with 2 litres (8½ cups) of water, bring to the boil and simmer for 1 hour.

Heat the olive oil in a large saucepan over a medium heat, add the chopped garlic, sliced leeks, onion, carrot, tomatoes and green pepper and sauté for a few minutes. Scoop your beans out with a slotted spoon (reserving the cooking liquid) and transfer them to the pan. Add the seasonings – salt, oregano, cumin, paprika, nutritional yeast and chillies – and stir, coating all of the ingredients.

Now add 1.25 litres (5 cups) of the bean cooking water to the pan and stir. Add the rice and cook for 20 minutes until tender, then serve.

The best dishes are a simple celebration of a single ingredient. This is a tribute to garlic. Try simply spreading it on toasted sourdough or fresh crusty bread for roasted garlic bread, or mashing it and adding it to cooked spaghetti.

Baked garlic

1 large garlic bulb, papery outer layers removed (skins of cloves left on)
2 tsp olive oil

Preheat the oven to 200°C/180°C Fan/400°F/gas 6.

Using a sharp knife, cut 1cm (½in) from the top of the garlic bulb, exposing the individual cloves.

Put the garlic bulb on a baking tray and drizzle the olive oil over the top, using your fingers to rub the oil over all the exposed garlic cloves. Cover the bulb with tin foil.

Bake for 30–40 minutes, or until the cloves are lightly browned and feel soft when pressed.

Remove from the oven and leave until it's cool enough to touch, then remove the roasted garlic cloves from their skins: use a knife to cut the skin slightly around each clove, then use your fingers to pull or squeeze the roasted garlic cloves out of their skins.

My childhood was littered with bubble-and-squeak Mondays made from Sunday dinner leftovers. This version is a variation of those childhood memories.

Bubble and squeak can be served in so many ways – I even used to eat it in sandwiches. It works perfectly with sausages, dark leafy greens and Vegetable Gravy (see page 33). Or simply add baked beans for a smaller meal.

Bubble and squeak

SERVES 2

1 tsp olive oil, for greasing
300g (10½oz) leftover mash (or 1 large potato, cooked and mashed)
1 carrot, grated
1 onion, thinly sliced
3 garlic cloves, thinly sliced
2 tbsp nutritional yeast
½ tsp sea salt
1 tsp freshly ground black pepper

Preheat the oven to 200°C/180°C Fan/400°F/gas 6 and grease a 20cm (8in) round baking tin or cake tin with oil.

Mix all the ingredients together in a bowl. Transfer to the greased tin and bake in the oven for 40 minutes until crispy and golden.

This leek and spinach pie is a real comfort-food dish. Try pairing it with the Slaw Salad (see page 80) and Waste-less Wedges (see page 128) for a real feast.

Leek and spinach pie

SERVES 4

Olive oil
1 onion, finely diced
2 leeks, thinly sliced
4 garlic cloves, finely chopped
½ tsp sea salt
1 tsp freshly ground black pepper
4 tbsp nutritional yeast
2 tsp dried basil
2 tsp dried parsley
700g (24½oz) frozen spinach (or fresh – non-bagged is best)
200ml (generous ¾ cup) vegan vegetable stock (made from a cube/powder, or see recipe on page 31)
320g (11½oz) pack chilled ready-rolled vegan puff pastry (or frozen pastry, thawed overnight in the fridge)

Heat a drizzle of olive oil in a large saucepan over a medium heat. Add the onion, leeks and garlic and sauté for a few minutes until the onion is translucent and the leeks have softened but not browned.

Add the salt, pepper, nutritional yeast and dried basil and parsley. Stir to coat the onions and leeks in the herbs, then add the spinach and stock. Increase the heat and let it bubble for 20 minutes, stirring occasionally, until the mixture has thickened and there is little moisture left. Remove from the heat.

Preheat the oven to 180°C/160°C Fan/350°F/gas 4 and line a baking tray with greaseproof paper.

Unroll your puff pastry on a work surface and cut it in half to make two squares. Place one half on the lined baking tray and spoon on the cooled filling, leaving a 5mm (⅛in) gap around the edge.

Place the other piece of pastry on top and press down the edges, sealing them in place. Brush with olive oil and bake in the oven for 45 minutes, until golden brown on top.

Remove from the oven and serve.

Puttanesca is a really common dish for anyone looking for simple, quick, delicious food. This puttanesca tart is even easier than the classic pasta dish.

Puttanesca tart

SERVES 4

320g (11½oz) pack chilled ready-rolled vegan puff pastry (or frozen pastry, thawed overnight in the fridge)
3 tbsp passata
Handful of grated vegan cheese (optional)
1 tbsp capers
1 fresh red chilli, finely diced
80g (½ cup) pitted black olives
50g (½ cup) sundried tomatoes in oil
A drizzle of olive oil
Sea salt and freshly ground black pepper
Rocket, cress, or other green leaf, to garnish (optional)

Preheat the oven to 200°C/180°C Fan/400°F/gas 6 and line a baking tray with greaseproof paprer.

Roll out the puff pastry on the lined baking tray and spread over the passata, leaving a 1cm (½in) gap around the edge. Sprinkle with the cheese, if using, then scatter on the rest of the ingredients. Drizzle with the olive oil and season with salt and pepper.

Bake in the oven for 25 minutes, until the pastry is golden brown, then remove from the oven and serve scattered with a green garnish of your choice, if using.

Garlic and mushroom is such a classic, delicious combination, and this buttery, decadent tart is an absolute winner for mushroom lovers. Don't worry about the fact that it looks like there are too many mushrooms — it will be perfect when baked.

Garlic mushroom tart

SERVES 2 AS A LIGHT LUNCH

320g (11½oz) pack chilled ready-rolled vegan puff pastry (or frozen pastry, thawed overnight in the fridge)

Handful of grated vegan cheese

3 garlic cloves, finely chopped

200g (3 cups) mushrooms, thinly sliced

Olive oil, for drizzling

½ tsp sea salt

1 tsp freshly ground black pepper

Handful of cress, rocket or chopped parsley (or greens of your choice), to garnish

Preheat the oven to 200°C/180°C Fan/400°F/gas 6 and line a baking tray with greaseproof paper.

Roll out the puff pastry on the lined baking tray and sprinkle it with the grated vegan cheese. Top with garlic and sliced mushrooms, then drizzle with olive oil and season with the salt and pepper.

Bake in the oven for 25 minutes until golden brown, then remove from the oven and top with a garnish of cress, rocket or parsley as a garnish.

Refried beans are my favourite part of Mexican cuisine. They aren't quick to make but I urge you to give this recipe a go and experience the pleasure of creating your own refried beans from scratch.

Refried beans

SERVES 8 AS A SIDE OR ACCOMPANIMENT

300g (1½ cups) pinto beans, soaked overnight or quick-soaked (see page 22), rinsed and drained
4 garlic cloves, peeled and left whole
2 tsp dried marjoram
Drizzle of olive oil
1 onion, finely diced
1 fresh red chilli, finely diced
1 tsp smoked paprika
1 tsp ground cumin
2 tsp sea salt

Put the beans, garlic and marjoram in a large pot, add 1.5 litres (6½ cups) of water and bring to the boil. Reduce the heat and simmer for 2 hours, until the beans are soft and you can mash one with the back of the spoon.

Heat a drizzle of olive oil in a large frying pan over a medium heat, then add the onion and chilli. Sauté for a few minutes until the onion softens and just starts to brown, then add the paprika, cumin and salt.

Use a slotted spoon to transfer the beans and garlic from the pot to the pan, making sure you save all of that water. Start to mash the beans using your spoon, a fork or a potato masher, until the mixture has a lumpy mashed consistency. Now start to ladle in some of the bean cooking water and continue to stir and mash over a very low heat until the refried beans have your desired thickness and smoothness – I like them slightly lumpy.

Chuna pasta is my plant-based alternative to seafood pasta. You can create those fishy, salty flavours without the need for actual fish.

Chuna pasta

SERVES 2

100g (1 cup) pasta shells
Drizzle of olive oil
1 fresh red chilli, finely
  chopped
4 garlic cloves, finely
  chopped
2 tbsp capers
1 × 400g (14oz) tin
  jackfruit, drained
  and rinsed
60g (½ cup) frozen peas
2 sheets of nori
Sea salt
Handful of grated vegan
  cheese (optional), to
  serve

Cook the pasta in a large saucepan of salted boiling water, following the packet instructions, then drain.

Heat the olive oil in a frying pan over a low heat, add the chilli and garlic and sauté gently for a couple of minutes until softened but not browned. Add the capers, jackfruit, cooked pasta and peas. Crumble the nori sheets into the pan, stir and warm through gently, then season with salt and serve warm, topped with the grated cheese (if using).

ONE POT

Real one-pot ragu
Red lentil dal
Cauliflower rice stir-fry
Ribollita
Easy vegan corn bread
Chilli, garlic and broccoli noodles
Lemon and pea risotto

I see a lot of one-pot recipes that tell you to add cooked pasta to the dish. Which begs the question: how many pots are we using here? This one-pot pasta is truly everything cooked in one pot. That means your spaghetti is going to soak up loads of delicious flavour.

Real one-pot ragu

SERVES 2

Drizzle of olive oil
200g (about 1 cup) frozen soy mince
100g (1½ cups) chestnut mushrooms, finely chopped
3 garlic cloves, finely chopped
1 fresh red chilli, finely chopped (or ½ tsp dried chilli flakes)
20g (¾oz) fresh sage, roughly chopped, or 2 tsp dried sage
500ml (2 cups) water or vegan vegetable stock (made from a cube/powder, or see recipe on page 31)
300ml (1¼ cups) passata
160g (5¾oz) tagliatelle
100g (1¾ cups) stale breadcrumbs
1 tsp freshly ground black pepper

Heat the oil in a large saucepan over a medium heat. Add the mince, mushrooms, garlic, chilli and sage and fry for a few minutes until the mushrooms have lost their liquid and softened, and the mince is slightly browned.

Add the water (or stock), add the passata and bring to a simmer. Add the tagliatelle and cook for 12 minutes. Sprinkle in breadcrumbs to soak up the excess moisture until you reach the desired thickness. Sprinkle with chopped herbs and stir them in. Serve sprinkled with the black pepper.

100

As a chef I find it extremely enticing to eat something different every day. However, this meal was so good I ate it every day for months while I perfected it. I go straight for dal when I yearn for simplicity and comfort.

Red lentil dal

SERVES 4

1 tsp coconut oil
6 garlic cloves, finely chopped
1 small brown onion, finely diced
1 small green chilli, finely chopped
½ tsp ground cardamom
½ tsp paprika
½ tsp ground cumin
½ tsp ground turmeric
Thumb-sized piece of fresh ginger, minced
2 tsp sea salt
1 ripe tomato, finely diced
190g (1 cup) red lentils, soaked in water for at least 1 hour, or overnight, drained and rinsed
Flatbreads, to serve (shop-bought or see recipe on page 125)

Heat the coconut oil in a large saucepan over a low heat, then add the garlic, onion and chilli. Sweat for a few minutes, then add your spices, ginger, salt and tomato. Stir and allow to stew for 5–10 minutes, until the tomato is completely broken down to mush. If the mixture becomes a little dry during this process add a few tablespoons of water.

Now it is time to add your lentils, which will have doubled in size while soaking. Add them to the pan and mix to combine with all of the tasty spices. Add 500ml (2 cups) water and stir. Pop the lid on, bring to the boil, then simmer for 20 minutes until thickened.

Remove from the heat and enjoy with flatbreads.

Cauliflower 'rice' is a great way to make use of your veggies and eat all the plants you can. The basic recipe for cauliflower rice is to pulse a head of cauliflower into a breadcrumb consistency in a food processor, then warm it and use it as a rice replacement, and here is my favourite way to use it.

Cauliflower rice stir-fry

SERVES 2

1 head of cauliflower, roughly broken into florets

2 tbsp reduced-sodium soy sauce

1 tbsp freshly grated ginger or 1 tsp ground ginger

2 tbsp sesame oil

2 garlic cloves, crushed

170g (6oz) broccoli florets, chopped

2 carrots, grated

150g (½ cup) frozen corn kernels or tinned, drained corn

130g (½ cup) frozen peas

4 tbsp hoisin sauce

½ tsp sesame seeds

2 spring onions, thinly sliced

To make the cauliflower rice, pulse the cauliflower in a food processor until it resembles rice.

In a small bowl, whisk together the soy sauce and ginger with half the sesame oil.

Heat the remaining sesame oil in a large frying pan or wok over a medium heat. Add the garlic and cook, stirring frequently, for 2 minutes, then stir in the broccoli, grated carrots, corn and peas and cook, stirring constantly, for a further 3–4 minutes until the vegetables are tender.

Stir in the cauliflower rice and soy sauce mixture and cook, stirring, for 3–4 minutes until everything is heated through and the cauliflower is tender.

Serve immediately, drizzled with the hoisin sauce and garnished with the sesame seeds and spring onions.

Ribollita, meaning to 're-boil', is perhaps the ultimate zero-waste creative dish. The recipe list might look long, but it's all about using up leftovers and store-cupboard ingredients, so shouldn't require a lengthy shopping trip.

Ribollita

SERVES 4

2 tbsp good-quality olive oil, plus extra to serve

1 onion, finely diced

1 carrot, diced

2 celery sticks, diced

6 garlic cloves, chopped

2 tsp sea salt

1 tsp black pepper

¼ tsp dried chilli flakes

4 tbsp nutritional yeast

1 × 400g (14oz) tin chopped tomatoes, or 2–3 tomatoes, diced

150g (5½oz) chopped cavolo nero or spinach

Splash of vegan white wine

750ml (3 cups) vegan vegetable stock (made from a cube/powder, or see recipe on page 31)

250g (1 cup) red beans or kidney beans, soaked overnight (or use 400g/14oz tinned), drained and rinsed

250g (1 cup) cannellini beans (soaked overnight or quick-soaked – see page 22), or tinned

15g (½ cup) chopped fresh parsley or 6g (¼ cup) dried parsley

120g (4½oz) stale bread, chopped or into pieces

Heat the olive oil in a large, heavy casserole dish over a low heat. Add the onion and sauté for 7–8 minutes, then add the carrot, celery, garlic, salt, pepper, chilli flakes and nutritional yeast. Cook for 10 minutes until the vegetables are tender.

Add the tomatoes and cavolo nero or spinach and the wine and sauté, stirring occasionally, for another 7–8 minutes.

Add the stock and beans, bring the soup to the boil, then reduce the heat back to low and simmer for 15–20 minutes until thickened.

Stir in the parsley and stale bread, then adjust the seasoning if necessary. Leave to stand for 5 minutes, then serve with olive oil and extra black pepper.

Corn bread is a delicious hearty bread that doesn't use any yeast. It is perfect for mopping up saucy dishes and is great to add to your repertoire of recipes.

Easy vegan corn bread

SERVES 4 AS A SIDE TO SOUPS AND STEWS

150g (1¼ cups) plain flour
120g (1 cup) yellow cornmeal
50g (¼ cup) granulated sugar
1 tsp sea salt
1 tbsp baking powder
300ml (1¼ cups) unsweetened almond milk (or plant-based milk of choice)
80ml (generous ⅓ cup) olive oil

Preheat the oven to 200°C/180°C Fan/400°F/gas 6 and line a 22cm (8.5in) square baking tin with greaseproof paper.

Mix the dry ingredients in a large mixing bowl, then add the wet ingredients and mix together until combined and smooth. Pour into the lined tin and bake in the oven for 25 minutes until golden brown.

Remove from the oven and leave to set for 30 minutes in the tin, then remove from the tin and leave to cool for a further 30 minutes before serving.

The corn bread is best eaten fresh, but can be stored in an airtight container at room temperature for up to 2–3 days.

I grew up loving cheap packet noodles full of goodness-knows-what. They were so simple to make and I've even been known to put them in sandwiches. Here I have created something a lot healthier and more satisfying.

Chilli, garlic and broccoli noodles

SERVES 2

2 tbsp vegetable or sesame oil
2 tbsp soy sauce
3 garlic cloves, finely chopped
1 fresh red chilli, finely chopped (or 1 tsp dried chilli flakes)
150g Tenderstem broccoli, halved (or a head of broccoli cut into small pieces)
1 tsp ground turmeric
1 tsp dried or fresh chopped thyme
1 tsp dried or fresh chopped parsley
1 tbsp nutritional yeast
250g (9oz) dried wholewheat noodles or noodles of choice (such as vermicelli)
Freshly ground black pepper

Heat the oil and soy sauce in a large saucepan over a low heat, add the garlic, chilli and broccoli and fry for a few minutes until softened. Add the turmeric, herbs and nutritional yeast and toss the broccoli in the seasoning.

Pour in 700ml (3 cups) water, increase the heat to high and add the noodles. Agitate the noodles to break them up as they soften and cook for a few minutes until completely cooked.

Season with black pepper and serve hot.

Lemon and pea is a great combination and this dish is a beautiful fresh lunch option. Try adding my Parmesan-style Topping on page 42 and shaved asparagus to take this dish up a notch.

Lemon and pea risotto

SERVES 4

200g (scant 1 cup) risotto rice
800ml (3¼ cups) hot vegan vegetable stock (cube/powdered, or see recipe on page 31)
75g (½ cup) garden peas
Handful of grated vegan cheese (optional)
Grated zest of 1 lemon and juice of ½
3 tbsp nutritional yeast
½ tsp sea salt
Freshly ground black pepper

Heat a large saucepan over a medium heat, then add the rice and toast the grains, stirring constantly, for 1 minute. Add a ladleful of the hot stock and stir until absorbed, then reduce the heat. Add the rest of the stock, a ladleful at a time, stirring after each addition until it's absorbed before adding the next ladle. Keep going until the rice is almost cooked and all the stock is absorbed – this will take about 20 minutes.

Stir in the peas and cook for 3–5 minutes, then remove the pan from the heat. Add the cheese, if using, and the lemon juice, nutritional yeast and salt, then stir. Scatter with the lemon zest and serve immediately with a good grinding of black pepper.

DINNER

Mushroom stroganoff
Italian-style toad-in-the-hole
Red lentil bolognese
Melanzane
Aubergine kebabs
Flatbread
Crumbed piri-piri sweet potato
Waste-less wedges
Pumpkin gnocchi
Stuffed cannelloni
Digger pie
Chuna linguine
Pizza-stuffed mushrooms
Pasta and salad
Sardinian risotto
Gnocchi alla romana
Aubergine rolls
Spicy sausage roll

Mushroom stroganoff is a delicious dish that was one of my favourites from the first restaurant I ever worked at. This delicious creamy tangy dish is one to add to your repertoire.

Mushroom stroganoff

SERVES 4

Drizzle of olive oil
3 shallots, finely
   chopped
2 garlic cloves, finely
   chopped
450g chestnut
   mushrooms,
   quartered
1 tsp smoked paprika
1 tsp dried chilli flakes
75ml (⅓ cup) vegan
   white wine
Juice of ½ lemon
1 tbsp Dijon mustard
200ml (generous ¾ cup)
   Oatly crème fraîche
Sea salt and freshly
   ground black pepper
15g fresh parsley,
   chopped, to serve

FOR THE RICE
270g (1⅓ cups) basmati
   rice, rinsed
1 lemongrass stalk,
   lightly bashed
1 cinnamon stick

Add the rice to a saucepan along with the aromatics and some salt and pepper. Pour in 500ml (2 cups) cold water, cover, bring to the boil and simmer for about 10 minutes until all the water has been absorbed. Remove from the heat, but keep it covered.

Heat the olive oil in a large saucepan over a medium heat and add the shallots, garlic and mushrooms. Sauté for 5 minutes until softened and the liquid from the mushrooms has evaporated, then stir in the paprika, chilli flakes and a large pinch of salt. Add the white wine and lemon juice and simmer for 5 minutes, stirring occasionally.

Stir the Dijon mustard and crème fraîche into the stroganoff to create a creamy, rich sauce. Season with salt and pepper. Remove the aromatics from the rice, fluff up the grains and serve alongside the stroganoff, garnished with parsley.

Toad-in-the-hole is a fantastic English classic but making
vegan Yorkshire pudding involves more science than cooking.
Why not try my easy polenta version to satisfy your cravings?

Italian-style toad-in-the-hole

SERVES 4

750ml (3 cups) water or
vegan vegetable stock
(made from a cube/
powder, or see recipe
on page 31)
1 tsp fine sea salt
160g (1 cup) coarse
polenta
2 tsp vegan butter
8 vegan sausages
Olive oil, for frying
1 red onion, thinly sliced

TO SERVE
Cooked dark leafy
greens
Vegetable Gravy (see
page 33)

Preheat the oven to 200°C/180°C Fan/400°F/gas
6 and line a 25 × 20cm (10 × 8in) roasting tin with
greaseproof paper.

Bring the water or stock and salt to the boil in a large
saucepan over a high heat. Pour in the polenta slowly,
whisking constantly, until all the polenta is stirred in
and there are no lumps. Add the butter, reduce the
heat to low and simmer, whisking often, for about 5
minutes until the polenta starts to thicken. Remove
from the heat and leave to rest for 5 minutes.

Pour the polenta mix into the lined tin and lay in your
vegan sausages. Drizzle with olive oil and bake in the
oven for 35 minutes, until the sausages are browned
and the polenta is darker in colour.

Meanwhile, heat a little oil in a frying pan and fry the
onions over a low heat for 10 minutes until soft and
starting to caramelise.

Serve the toad-in-the-hole topped with the fried
onions and with dark leafy greens and gravy.

Lentils are one of the most common store-cupboard items, and this cross between bolognese, dal and lasagne makes great use of them. This recipe is endlessly adaptable, so feel free to mix it up; try adding dried chilli flakes or courgette, more or less garlic, or switch the lentils for finely chopped mushrooms.

Red lentil bolognese

SERVES 4

1 tbsp olive oil
4 garlic cloves, finely chopped or crushed
1 small onion, finely diced
1 celery stick, finely chopped
1 carrot, finely chopped
2 tsp dried rosemary
1 tsp dried oregano
1 tsp dried basil
1 tsp sea salt
100ml (scant ½ cup) vegan red wine (optional)
190g (1 cup) red lentils, soaked in water for at least 1 hour, or overnight, then drained and rinsed
1 × 400g (14oz) tin chopped tomatoes
1 vegan vegetarian stock cube (optional)
Cooked pasta or diced roasted potatoes, to serve

Heat the olive oil in a saucepan over a low heat, add the garlic, onion, celery and carrot and cook, covered, for a few minutes until softened. Add the herbs and salt. If you're using wine, add it now and cook for a further couple of minutes, otherwise go straight in with the lentils (which will have doubled in size while soaking), tomatoes and half a tin (200ml/ generous ¾ cup) water (this not only adds moisture but it makes sure you don't waste the tomatoes stuck to the sides of the tin – perfect if you're trying to reduce waste, or are cheap like me!).

Crumble in the stock cube, if using, increase the heat, stir and wait until the liquid is bubbling, then reduce the heat and simmer, uncovered, for 30 minutes until you have a rich, thick sauce and the lentils have softened.

Serve with pasta or diced roasted potatoes.

Melanzane, an Italian dish of layers of aubergine with a rich tomato sauce topped with cheese and breadcrumbs, is a really tasty, healthy way of celebrating the aubergine. Delicious!

Melanzane

SERVES 4

Drizzle of olive oil
5 garlic cloves, finely chopped
1 onion, finely diced
2 tsp dried oregano
1 × 400g (14oz) tin plum tomatoes
3 aubergines, tops removed, cut into 5mm (⅛in)-thick slices (lengthways or into circular discs)
Handful of fresh basil leaves
5 tbsp polenta or breadcrumbs
150g (5½oz) grated vegan cheese (optional)
Sea salt and freshly ground black pepper
Garlic bread and fresh salad, to serve

Preheat the oven to 200°C/180°C Fan/400°F/gas 6.

Heat the olive oil in a large saucepan over a low heat. Add the garlic and onion and cook for a few minutes until the onion begins to soften, then add the dried oregano, season with salt and pepper and stir. Tip in the plum tomatoes and use the back of a wooden spoon to crush them as you simmer for 10 minutes. Cover and set the sauce to one side.

Heat a griddle (ribbed skillet) or frying pan over a high heat (a ribbed pan works best, as it gives you the lines when you grill the aubergine). Place a batch of aubergine slices in the pan and cook for about a minute until slightly charred, then turn them over with tongs and grill on the other side until both sides are lightly charred. Remove and repeat with another batch of sliced aubergine until you have charred all of the slices.

To assemble the melanzane, first spoon some sauce onto the base of a baking dish and use the back of the spoon to smooth it out, coating the dish. Lay slices of charred aubergine over the sauce until you have one full layer, closing gaps with aubergine where possible. Spoon on your next layer of sauce and add some roughly torn basil leaves and lightly sprinkle with a tablespoon of polenta or breadcrumbs. Add the next layer of aubergine and repeat the layering until you have used all of the aubergine, finishing with the breadcrumbs and the grated cheese (if using).

Bake in the oven for 35 minutes, then serve with garlic bread and a fresh side salad.

Kebabs are not just for nights out and BBQs. These plant-based aubergine kebabs are a delicious option for any meal. Adjust the hot sauce to meet your desired level of heat or try swapping it for BBQ sauce if you prefer.

Aubergine kebabs

SERVES 4

FOR THE KEBABS
100ml (scant ½ cup) hot sauce
3 tbsp olive oil
6 tbsp golden syrup
2 tbsp lemon juice
2 aubergines (2 kebabs per aubergine)

TO SERVE
4 flatbreads (shop-bought, or see opposite)
Romaine or iceberg lettuce, roughly chopped
2 tomatoes, thinly sliced
1 red onion, thinly sliced

Preheat the oven to 200°C/180°C Fan/400°F/gas 6 and line a baking tray with greaseproof paper.

Combine the hot sauce, olive oil, golden syrup and lemon juice in a mixing bowl and set to one side.

Slice the aubergines into the thinnest rounds you can manage; the thinner you slice the aubergine the more marinade you will get on each slice and the crispier the edges will be when cooked.

Coat all the aubergine slices in the marinade and fold each slice in half before skewering onto a kebab skewer – you will need about four skewers.

Place the skewers on the lined baking tray and bake in the oven for 40 minutes until crispy.

Serve the kebabs on flatbreads with lettuce, tomato and red onion.

Flatbreads are the oldest type of bread. A style of bread made without yeast, at its most basic form it contains only flour and water. These flatbreads are a little more decadent and fluffy. Enjoy them with soups, stews and for serving with kebabs.

Flatbread

MAKES 4 FLATBREADS

180g (1½ cups) self-raising flour, plus extra for dusting
1 tsp sea salt
1 tsp baking powder
150g (generous ⅓ cup) natural vegan yoghurt (or 80ml/⅓ cup water)
Olive oil, for brushing

Mix the flour, salt and baking powder together in a bowl, then add the yoghurt and knead together until just combined. Cover the bowl with a clean tea towel and leave in a warm spot for 1 hour.

Warm a frying pan or griddle pan (ribbed skillet) over a high heat.

Cut the flatbread dough into quarters and press each piece until it's 5mm (⅛in) thick. Brush the top of the flatbreads with olive oil, then lay them oiled-side down on the pan, two at a time. Brush the other side with oil and cook for 2 minutes on each side, turning them with tongs, until risen and lightly charred.

Spiced sweet potato is delicious with or without the breadcrumbs, so feel free to leave them out if you are avoiding gluten or just trying to cut calories.

Crumbed piri-piri sweet potato

SERVES 4

30g (½ cup)
   breadcrumbs
1 tbsp piri piri seasoning
Pinch of sea salt
2 sweet potatoes,
   washed (skin on) and
   cut into 1.5cm (¾in)-
   thick slices
1 tbsp olive oil
Cooked green beans
   or cauliflower rice,
   to serve

Preheat the oven to 180°C/160°C Fan/350°F/gas 4 and line a baking tray with greaseproof paper.

Mix together the breadcrumbs, piri piri seasoning and salt on a plate. Coat the slices of sweet potato in the olive oil, then coat them in the seasoned breadcrumb mixture.

Spread the potato slices out on the lined baking tray and bake in the oven for 50 minutes, until darkened and crispy.

Remove from the oven and serve with green beans or cauliflower rice.

Potatoes are one of the most versatile ingredients in the kitchen, so why do we often neglect and waste them? Try making these waste-less wedges, or use them to make mash, gnocchi, a gratin, tater tots, hash browns, dauphinoise, duchess potatoes, croquettes, boil them for a potato salad, turn them into chips or – of course – roasties.

These are perfect served with the Aubergine Kebabs on page 124 or Spicy Sausage Roll on page 146.

Waste-less wedges

SERVES 4 AS A SIDE

600g baking potatoes, scrubbed and cut into wedges – about 8 wedges per potato (unpeeled)
Glug of olive oil
1 tsp sea salt
1 tsp freshly ground black pepper
1 tsp dried oregano
1 tsp smoked paprika
1 tsp dried chilli flakes

Preheat the oven to 200°C/180°C Fan/400°F/gas 6.

Put the potato wedges in a large bowl, add the olive oil and toss to coat. Combine the salt, pepper, oregano and spices, then add to the wedges and toss together again.

Tip the wedges onto a large baking tray and spread them out in one layer. Roast in the oven for 40 minutes, until golden, crisp and cooked through.

Potatoes are hugely wasted and so are pumpkins. It is estimated that 8 million pumpkins get wasted each year in Britain alone, yet every part of a pumpkin is actually edible (yes, even the stem). Try this recipe if you really must carve a pumpkin this year.

I like to pan-fry my gnocchi with olive oil, chilli, sage and wilted spinach, but you can also poach them for a few minutes in salted boiling water, remove with a slotted spoon and enjoy with any sauce you like. I recommend a potato ricer for this recipe but if you don't have one you can use a masher.

Pumpkin gnocchi

SERVES 4

1 otherwise-wasted
    pumpkin, peeled,
    deseeded and cubed
    (250g/9oz prepared
    weight)
Pinch of sea salt
350g (2¾ cups) plain
    flour, plus extra for
    dusting
Drizzle of olive oil
1 fresh red chilli, finely
    chopped
3 garlic cloves, finely
    chopped
40g fresh sage leaves,
    roughly chopped, or
    3 tsp dried sage
3 handfuls of spinach
    (non-bagged is best)

Preheat the oven to 180°C/160°C Fan/350°F/gas 4 and line a baking tray with greaseproof paper.

Spread the cubed pumpkin out on the lined baking tray and roast in the oven for 50 minutes until softened. Remove from the oven and leave to cool.

Dust a work surface with flour, then pop the cooled roasted pumpkin into a potato ricer and squeeze them onto the floured surface. (Alternatively, mash the pumpkin until smooth and place it on the floured surface.)

Sprinkle the salt over the pumpkin and dust it with half the flour, then begin to knead it all together. Gradually add more of the remaining flour, bit by bit, until your dough is no longer sticky (you may not need all the flour). Form the dough into a ball, then divide it into quarters.

RECIPE CONTINUES ON NEXT PAGE

RECIPE CONTINUED FROM PREVIOUS PAGE

Roll each piece of dough into a long sausage shape roughly the width of two fingers. Work your way down the 'sausage', cutting pieces of dough at thumb-width intervals, then rolling each piece between your thumb and forefinger to produce an oval shape. Feel free to use the back of a fork to add ridges to the gnocchi if you like. The more ridges and curves they have, the more sauce they will carry.

Heat the olive oil in a frying pan over a medium heat. Add the chilli and garlic and fry for a minute or two until softened, then add the sage and gnocchi and fry for 5 minutes until they start to brown. Add the spinach and cook for a further minute or two until wilted, then remove from the heat and serve.

This cannelloni is a rich dish made with vegan mince and mushrooms, creating a comforting, flavourful meal. Cannelloni is a beautiful dish, perfect for preparing ahead of time and freezing. You can stuff the tubes with the filling and freeze them in tubs, ready for a quick mid-week dinner (defrost before baking).

You may want to use a piping bag for filling the tubes, though it's not essential.

Stuffed cannelloni

SERVES 2

Drizzle of olive oil

3 garlic cloves, finely chopped

200g (3 cups) mushrooms, very finely chopped

200g (1 cup) frozen soy mince

1 tsp dried oregano

Pinch of sea salt

1 tsp freshly ground black pepper

200ml (generous ¾ cup) vegan vegetable stock (made from a cube/ powder, or see recipe on page 31)

200ml (generous ¾ cup) passata

14 dried cannelloni tubes

Handful of grated vegan cheese

Light salad, to serve

Preheat the oven to 200°C/180°C Fan/400°F/gas 6 and line the base and sides of a 2lb loaf tin with greaseproof paper.

Heat the olive oil in a large saucepan over a medium heat, add the garlic, mushrooms and soy mince and sauté for 10 minutes until the mushrooms have shrunk and the mince has softened and cooked. Add the oregano, salt, pepper, stock and passata. Stir and simmer for a further 10 minutes until thickened slightly.

Stuff the cannelloni tubes with the filling, making sure you have some filling mixture left over. You can do this with a piping bag fitted with a large nozzle or by carefully spooning it into the tubes.

Sprinkle half the cheese into the base of the loaf tin and start to layer the stuffed cannelloni on top.

When you have filled the tin, spoon on the rest of the filling and sprinkle with the remaining cheese. Pop it into the oven to bake for 20 minutes, or until the cheese has melted and the pasta is al dente.

Enjoy with a light salad.

When I was at school, we were blessed with a dish called 'digger pie' and it was always the highlight of my week. Digger pie was usually made using lamb mince but it is so simple to make an easy swap to vegan mince. The tasty savoury stew is topped with a suet pastry crust; it's a beautiful variation of stew and dumplings. Serve with mashed potatoes and gravy.

Digger pie

SERVES 4

Drizzle of olive oil
250g (1¼ cups) frozen
    vegan soy mince
2 garlic cloves, finely
    chopped
2 carrots, diced
1 potato, diced
2 tsp freshly ground
    black pepper
550ml (2⅓cups) vegan
    stock (cube/powdered,
    or see page 31)
200g (scant 2 cups)
    frozen peas

FOR THE SUET PASTRY CRUST
100g (3½oz) vegan suet
200g (1⅔ cups) self-
    raising flour, plus extra
    for dusting
Pinch of sea salt

TO SERVE
Mashed potatoes
Vegetable Gravy
    (see page 33)

Preheat the oven to 180°C/160°C Fan/350°F/gas 4.

Heat the olive oil in an ovenproof casserole dish over a medium heat, add the frozen mince, garlic, carrots and potato and sauté for a few minutes, then add the pepper and stir in the stock and frozen peas. Reduce the heat to low and keep warm.

Combine the suet, self-raising flour and salt in a bowl and use your fingertips to rub them together to form a crumb. Gradually add 150ml (⅔cup) cold water and work the water into the mixture using your hands to create a dough.

Dust a work surface with flour and roll out the dough to a flat, smooth circle slightly smaller than the diameter of the pie dish you are using.

Transfer the pie mixture to the pie dish and carefully place the dough on top. Brush it with some of the liquid from the stew, then pinch the edges to the tin to seal. Bake in the oven for 40 minutes until golden brown, then remove from the oven and serve with mash and gravy.

Jackfruit is incredibly versatile, not only for using as a pulled pork alternative but as a tuna substitute, too. Try this 'chuna' linguine for a vegan take on an authentic Italian dish.

Chuna linguine

SERVES 4

350g (12½oz) dried
   linguine (100 per cent
   durum wheat), or
   spaghetti or tagliatelle
2 tbsp olive oil
Small bunch of fresh
   parsley, finely
   chopped
3 garlic cloves, finely
   chopped
3 tbsp capers
2 tsp dried chilli flakes
1 × 400g (14oz) tin
   young jackfruit,
   drained and rinsed
250ml (1 cup) passata
Sea salt and freshly
   ground black pepper

Cook the linguine in a large saucepan of salted boiling water for 5 minutes less than the time stated on the packet.

Heat the olive oil in a large frying pan over a medium heat and add half of the chopped parsley, along with the garlic, capers and dried chilli flakes. Sauté for a few minutes until the garlic is soft, then add the jackfruit and break it into chunks with a wooden spoon. Season with salt and pepper, add the passata and stir to combine.

Add a ladle of water from the pasta pan to the sauce, then transfer all of the pasta to the pan with tongs. Stir to coat the pasta in the sauce and simmer for a further 4 minutes before serving.

Portobello mushrooms are a beautiful, tasty vessel for flavour. Try preparing these stuffed 'shrooms ahead of time, ready for a delicious, impressive-looking meal any time you choose.

Pizza-stuffed mushrooms

SERVES 4 AS A STARTER

8 portobello mushrooms
150g (5½oz) vegan cheese, grated
100ml (scant ½ cup) passata
100g (1¼ cups) dried coarse breadcrumbs
3 tbsp olive oil
2 fresh red chillies, finely chopped
4 garlic cloves, finely chopped
2 tsp dried oregano
Sea salt and freshly ground black pepper

Preheat the oven to 180°C/160°C Fan/350°F/gas 4 and line a baking tray with greaseproof paper.

Remove the stalks from the portobello mushrooms and place the mushrooms upside down on the lined baking tray.

Combine all the remaining ingredients in a mixing bowl and season with salt and pepper. Spoon the mixture evenly into each mushroom, until all of the mixture has been used up, then bake in the oven for 20 minutes, until the filling is bubbling and lightly browned on top.

Remove from the oven and serve warm.

Salad is usually served on its own, or as a light lunch, however, combining salad with pasta (this is nothing like the pasta salad I made at school) is a great way to reduce your portion of pasta, increase your greens and not feel restricted. It couldn't be simpler.

Pasta and salad

SERVES 2

100g (3½oz) dried
    orecchiette
1 romaine lettuce head,
    roughly chopped
150g (5½oz) cherry
    tomatoes, halved
1 courgette, grated
1 tbsp olive oil
25g fresh basil leaves,
    torn
2 tbsp chopped nuts
    (either Brazil nuts,
    pine nuts or cashews)
Grated zest and juice of
    1 lemon

Cook the orecchiette in a large saucepan of salted boiling water, following the packet instructions, until al dente, then drain and return the pasta back to the warm pan with all of the other ingredients. Stir, pop the lid on and leave for 5 minutes to gently warm all the other ingredients before serving.

Sardinian risotto is a hearty rice dish prepared by cooking the rice in a flavourful ragu-style sauce, which gives the rice a deep, rich flavour. Try cooking twice the amount and using half to make arancini, or my Aubergine Rolls on page 144.

Sardinian risotto

SERVES 4

Drizzle of olive oil
500g (generous 2 cups) risotto rice
700ml (3 cups) vegan vegetable stock (made from a cube/powder, or see recipe on page 31)
4 tbsp Parmesan-style Topping (see page 42), to serve

FOR THE SAUCE
Olive oil
1 small onion, finely chopped
200g (1 cup) frozen vegan soy mince or vegan sausages, crumbled
1 small glass of vegan red wine (about 150ml/⅔ cup)
250ml (1 cup) passata
Sea salt

To make the sauce, heat the olive oil in a large saucepan over a medium heat, add the onion and gently sauté for a few minutes until softened. Add the mince or crumbled vegan sausages and fry for 10 minutes over a low heat until it has softened and slightly darkened. Pour in the wine and passata and stir, then simmer for 15 minutes.

Heat some olive oil in a large saucepan over a medium heat. Tip in the risotto rice and stir, coating it in the oil and lightly toasting it for about 3 minutes.

Add two ladles of stock into the rice and simmer until it has absorbed most of the liquid. Now add another ladle and repeat until you have used all of the stock.

Now add the sauce mixture, stir and simmer for 10 minutes, stirring regularly, to make sure it doesn't catch on the base of the pan. Turn off the heat and leave to rest for 5 minutes.

Sprinkle with Parmesan-style topping and serve.

Gnocchi alla romana is traditionally made using semolina, however this chickpea (gram) flour version packs in even more flavour. It is perfect paired with an arrabbiata sauce.

Gnocchi alla romana

SERVES 4

Small bunch of fresh parsley, finely chopped
Large pinch of salt
250g (generous 1¾ cups) chickpea (gram) flour (check the use-by date, as it needs to be as fresh as possible)
Olive oil, for greasing and drizzling
80g (¾ cup) sundried tomatoes in oil
5 tbsp Parmesan-style Topping (see page 42)
Grated zest of 1 lemon (lemon then cut into wedges)
1 tsp ground nutmeg
Freshly ground black pepper

Line a 15 × 30cm (6 × 12in) baking tray with greaseproof paper.

Bring 800ml (3¼ cups) water to the boil in a large saucepan with the parsley and salt. Gradually add the chickpea (gram) flour and whisk to mix together and prevent lumps. Cook for 5 minutes over a high heat, stirring constantly, until smooth and combined, then pour onto the lined baking tray and leave to cool and set. This should take 40–60 minutes in the fridge.

Preheat the oven to 200°C/180°C Fan/400°F/gas 6. Tip the gnocchi mixture onto a clean chopping board and grease the baking tray you used for chilling the gnocchi with oil (to save on washing up).

Slice the gnocchi into rectangles 1cm x 5mm (½ x ⅛in) or use a 2cm (¾in) circular cutter to cut small circles. Lay them on the greased baking tray – they can slightly overlap, so don't worry about being too precise. Bake the gnocchi in the oven for 40 minutes.

RECIPE CONTINUES ON NEXT PAGE

FOR THE ARRABBIATA SAUCE

3 tbsp vegan butter or extra virgin olive oil

4 large garlic cloves, crushed

2 tsp dried chilli flakes, or 2 fresh red chillies, deseeded and finely chopped

25g fresh basil leaves, torn or roughly chopped, or 2 tbsp dried basil

1 × 400g (14oz) tin plum tomatoes

½ tsp sea salt

½ tsp freshly cracked black pepper

Remove the tray from the oven and fill the gaps with the sundried tomatoes. Drizzle lightly with olive oil and scatter with the Parmesan-style topping, lemon zest, nutmeg and some black pepper. Bake for a further 5 minutes until the gnocchi are crispy, then remove from the oven.

To make the arrabbiata sauce, heat the butter or oil in a small saucepan over a medium heat. Add the garlic and chilli and sauté for a minute until the garlic has begun to soften, then add the basil, tomatoes, salt and pepper and simmer for 10 minutes until thickened.

Plate up the gnocchi, smother with the sauce and serve with lemon wedges.

Aubergine rolls are traditionally like a fancy, delicate version of Melanzane (see page 121). They are a little more time-consuming to make, but the wow-factor pay-off is huge. Think about your aubergine rolls like sandwiches, and don't be limited to the options I am giving here: run off and experiment with leftovers to create something magic, such as stuffing the aubergine with pasta in arrabbiata sauce (see page 140) or making mac and cheese aubergine rolls. You will need 10 toothpicks.

Aubergine rolls

SERVES 4 AS A SIDE OR STARTER

2 large aubergines
400g (14oz) leftover Sardinian Risotto (see page 138) (about 1 tbsp for each roll)
10 sundried tomatoes in oil
10 large green olives
Drizzle of olive oil
½ lemon

Preheat the oven to 180°C/160°C Fan/350°F/gas 4.

Cut each aubergine into 5 × 5mm (⅛in)-thick slices (save the ends to use in another recipe, such as caponata), using a sharp, steady knife or a mandoline.

Heat a griddle pan (ribbed skillet) over a high heat and char each slice of aubergine briefly for about 30 seconds each side, until softened and browned in places, removing them with tongs.

Spoon about 1 tablespoon of the risotto into the centre of each aubergine slice and fold the ends of the aubergine over the filling. Gently turn the roll upside down to hide the folds and skewer with a toothpick to hold them in place. Lay all the rolls on a baking tray and coat lightly with a drizzle of olive oil and a squeeze of lemon juice.

Cook in the oven for 20 minutes, then remove from the oven and skewer a sundried tomato and olive on each roll. Serve warm.

This Wellington-style spicy sausage roll creates a spectacular roast dinner, and makes the perfect centrepiece to wow your friends and family. Serve with a creamy sauce (such as my Cheesy Mustard Sauce on page 37) and dark leafy greens.

Spicy sausage roll

SERVES 4

200g (3 cups) mushrooms
2 fresh red chillies, finely chopped
1 tsp smoked paprika
Grated zest and juice of 1 orange
270g (9½oz) pack vegan sausages (defrosted if frozen)
50g (1 cup) fresh breadcrumbs
320g (11½oz) pack chilled ready-rolled vegan puff pastry (or frozen pastry, thawed overnight in the fridge)
Plant-based milk, for brushing
2 tsp freshly ground black pepper
Pinch of flaky sea salt

TO SERVE
Cheesy Mustard Sauce (page 37)
Cooked dark leafy greens

Preheat the oven to 200°C/180°C Fan/400°F/gas 6 and line a baking tray with greaseproof paper.

Blitz the mushrooms in a food processor (taking care not to purée them), or finely chop them by hand. Transfer to a bowl and add the chillies, paprika, orange zest and juice, sausages and breadcrumbs and combine using your hands.

Unroll the puff pastry onto the lined baking tray. Form the mixture into a fat sausage shape just shorter than the length of the pastry rectangle. Place the sausage on the pastry and fold the pastry over it, pinching the sides to encase the sausage. Take a sharp knife and score the top of the sausage roll with diagonal slits. Brush the top of the roll with plant-based milk and season with black pepper and salt.

Bake the sausage roll in the oven for 25 minutes until golden brown and crisp.

Remove from the oven and serve with a creamy sauce and dark leafy greens.

DESSERT

Peanut butter cookies
Banana custard tarts
Banana nice cream
Churros
Churros dipping sauces

Salted caramel sauce | Thick chocolate sauce
Cinnamon bun frosting

Shortbread biscuits
Strawberry jam apple pies
Fridge cake
Rum and ginger cake
Dark chocolate tahini brownies
Raw cookie dough bar
Pineapple upside-down cake
Tepache
Fruity bread pudding
Easy vegan spotted dick
Tiramisu
Amaretti biscuits
Easy vegan treacle sponge

I considered it a huge privilege to get the chance to bake with my grandparents. My nan would delegate jobs to all of her grandchildren: measuring the flour, adding the sugar, spooning in peanut butter, pouring in the milk. We all got messy but it was worth it for those sweet treats from the oven.

Peanut butter cookies

MAKES 12 COOKIES

120g (4½oz) vegan butter, unsalted or salted, at room temperature

120g (scant ⅔ cup) brown sugar

¼ tsp sea salt

150g (1¼ cups) plain flour

1 tsp baking powder

150g (scant ⅔ cup) peanut butter (smooth or crunchy), gently warmed so it's runnier

40g (¼ cup) peanut halves

Put the butter, brown sugar and salt in a bowl and beat together until combined.

Sift the flour and baking powder into a separate bowl, then combine it with the butter and sugar mixture, then fold in the warmed peanut butter.

Once combined, cover and chill in the fridge for 1 hour until firm.

Preheat the oven to 180°C/160°C Fan/350°F/gas 4 and line a baking tray with greaseproof paper.

Use a spoon to transfer chunks of the dough onto the lined baking tray, rolling the chunks into 12 balls half the size of a golf ball and then lightly press them with three fingers. Space them out, as they will expand in the oven as they bake.

Sprinkle each cookie with a few peanut halves then bake in the oven for 15 minutes until golden brown. Remove from the oven and leave to cool slightly, then transfer to a wire rack to cool for 30 minutes and enjoy with a cup of tea.

The cookies will keep well, stored in an airtight container, for up to 3–5 days.

Banana and custard is one of my favourite pairings. I asked for it all the time as a child. These banana custard tarts are a real throwback to childhood.

You will need two 12-hole muffin tins.

Banana custard tarts

MAKES 12 TARTS

FOR THE PASTRY
(or use 320g pack ready-made shortcrust)
150g (1¼ cups) plain flour, plus extra for dusting
½ tsp fine sea salt
50ml (scant ¼ cup) sunflower oil, plus extra for greasing

FOR THE FILLING
2 tbsp custard powder
2 tbsp caster sugar
550ml (2⅓ cups) oat milk (shop-bought or see recipe on page 34)
4 ripe bananas, sliced
Pinch of ground turmeric (optional)
Pinch of grated nutmeg for each tart

Preheat the oven to 180°C/160°C Fan/350°F/gas 4 and grease a 12-hole muffin tin with oil.

To make the pastry, mix the flour and salt together in a large bowl. Add the sunflower oil and rub it into the flour using your fingertips, until the mixture resembles rough breadcrumbs. Add 3 tablespoons of cold water and mix with a spoon until the dough comes together to form a ball. Wrap it in clingfilm and chill in the fridge for 1 hour.

Very lightly dust a work surface with flour. Dust a rolling pin with a little more flour, then roll out the dough to a thickness of 2–3mm (⅛in). Cut into 12 discs to fit your muffin tin. Gently place another muffin tin on top and blind-bake in the oven for 15 minutes until firm. Remove the top tray and bake for a further 10 minutes until the pastry is golden brown. Remove from the oven and set aside to cool.

To make the filling, mix the custard powder and sugar in a saucepan. Add 2 tablespoons of the milk and combine to make a smooth paste, before adding the rest of the milk. Heat gently, stirring continuously, until simmering. Remove from the heat and set aside to cool for 30 minutes.

Spoon the custard filling into the baked pastry shells and top with sliced bananas.

Refrigerate for 1 hour before eating, then sprinkle with the turmeric (if using) and nutmeg.

My favourite flavour of banana 'nice' cream is chocolate and peanut butter. Like all 'nice' cream, it is really quick to make and you can eat it instantly. If you want to be able to scoop it, pour it into a lined loaf tin and pop it in the freezer for an hour, then it will be firmer and ready to scoop.

Banana nice cream

SERVES 2

3 frozen peeled bananas
6 tbsp cocoa powder
4 tbsp smooth peanut butter
A little plant-based milk, if needed
Toppings of choice, to serve (such as berries, crushed nuts or broken biscuit)

Put all of the ingredients in a blender or food processor and blend until smooth – you may need to add a little bit of plant-based milk to get the ingredients to combine. If you do need to do this, add a little bit at a time, as adding too much will create more of a smoothie consistency than a 'nice' cream one. Pour it into a bowl, add your favourite toppings and enjoy right away.

Churros are such a decadent, delicious treat. You can try making your own coatings and toppings, such as melted chocolate or sprinkles, but here I have opted for the classic cinnamon and sugar coating, with dip options and a frosting recipe on page 161. Enjoy!

You will need a large piping bag with a large star nozzle, and ideally a thermometer.

Churros

MAKES 12 CHURROS

200g (scant 1 cup)
   caster sugar, plus
   2 tbsp for dusting
½ tsp sea
½ tsp vanilla extract
1–1.5 litres (4–6½ cups)
   vegetable oil
240g (2 cups) plain flour
4 tbsp ground cinnamon

Combine 500ml (2 cups) water with the sugar, salt, vanilla extract and 2 tablespoons of the vegetable oil in a medium saucepan. Place over a medium heat, stir to combine and bring to the boil, then remove from the heat.

Tip in the flour and beat with a wooden spoon, making sure all of the flour is completely mixed in. Leave the dough to cool for about 15 minutes.

Transfer your cooled dough to a large piping bag fitted with a large star nozzle and place it in the fridge to cool for an extra 30 minutes.

Heat the remaining vegetable oil in a large saucepan to 350°F (180°C), adjusting the amount of oil depending on the size of your pan. Adjust the heat to keep the oil at a constant temperature during frying. If you don't have a thermometer, test some of the churros mixture to see if the oil is hot enough – it should start to bubble around the dough immediately and the dough should quickly start to transition to a golden brown crispy texture.

Very carefully pipe a few 10cm (4in)-long churros into the hot oil and fry for 4–5 minutes until they are crispy and golden brown, turning them gently with tongs to ensure they brown evenly.

Using a slotted spoon, remove the churros from the oil and let them drain on kitchen paper. Repeat with the rest of the churros mixture.

Combine the remaining 2 tablespoons of sugar with the cinnamon in a large bowl. Toss the warm churros around the bowl to coat, then serve.

Churros dipping sauces

MAKES ENOUGH FOR 4 SAUCE POTS (EACH IS ENOUGH FOR 12 CHURROS)
You can double this recipe and store the salted caramel in a sterilised jar in the fridge for up to 1 month, then you'll have this amazing sauce to hand for any sweet-tooth moments.

Salted caramel sauce

100g (generous 1 cup) light brown muscovado sugar
1 × 150ml (⅔ cup) tin full-fat coconut milk
20g (¾oz) vegan butter
2 tsp vanilla extract
½ tsp sea salt

Put the sugar and coconut milk in a saucepan over a low heat and stir until fully combined. Bring to the boil, then simmer vigorously for 15 minutes, stirring occasionally, until thickened and slightly reduced.

Remove from the heat and whisk in the vegan butter, vanilla extract and salt. Pour into a sterilised jar and leave to cool; the sauce will thicken slightly as it cools.

Serve in small pots with the churros.

A thick chocolate sauce is a classic and delicious way to compliment your churros. Dipping them is all part of the fun. This recipe only needs two ingredients and two steps – simple is always best.

Thick chocolate sauce

200g (7oz) vegan dark chocolate, chopped
50ml (scant ¼ cup) soy or oat cream

Put the chocolate in a saucepan over a very low heat for a few moments until it starts to soften and melt. Stir until the chocolate melts completely, keeping the heat very low. For anyone worried about the chocolate catching and burning in the heat, you can use the bain-marie method: simply place a little water in a saucepan, bring to a simmer over a gentle heat, place a heatproof glass bowl over the pan (making sure it doesn't touch the water) and place the chocolate in the bowl.

Remove the bowl of melted chocolate from the heat, pour in the cream and stir until the chocolate has completely combined. Add more vegan cream if you want to make a chocolate sauce that's a bit runnier.

Churros and cinnamon buns have a lot in common with their sweet cinnamon flavour combo, so why not try this amazing frosting and turn your churros into a stick of cinnamon-bun awesomeness?

Cinnamon bun frosting

250g (9oz) vegan unsalted butter, softened
1 tsp vanilla extract
175g (1½ cups) icing sugar

Put the softened vegan butter in a large mixing bowl and use an electric handheld whisk or stand mixer to cream it until the butter is smooth and fluffy. Add the vanilla and mix to combine, then start to add the icing sugar, half a cup (60g) at a time, until the frosting has reached your desired thickness. Use a spatula to carefully scrap down any mixture that has stuck to the side of the bowl, to make sure that everything is evenly mixed.

Once the frosting is ready you can serve it either in a dipping tub or spoon the mixture into a piping bag fitted with a large nozzle and pipe the mixture onto the cinnamon-covered churros to create a cinnamon-bun effect.

I was first taught how to make shortbread biscuits at school. I couldn't believe how simple the recipe was or how easy they were to make. This is a perfect recipe for making with children or for whipping up quickly to impress guests. Try melting a large bar of chocolate and dipping half of each biscuit in the chocolate once they have cooled, placing them on greaseproof paper to set – it really takes them to the next level.

Shortbread biscuits

MAKES 12 BISCUITS

150g (1¼ cups) plain flour, plus extra for dusting
100g (3½oz) vegan butter, softened
50g (¼ cup) granulated sugar, plus extra for sprinkling

Combine all the ingredients in a bowl until you have a smooth biscuit dough. Wrap in clingfilm and chill in the fridge for 30 minutes.

Roll out the chilled dough on a work surface lightly dusted with flour to a thickness of about 1.5cm (¾in) then cut into shapes with a cutter. Place the shapes on a greaseproof paper-lined baking tray, sprinkle with sugar and chill in the fridge for 20 minutes. Preheat the oven to 180°C/160°C Fan/350°F/gas 4.

Bake in the oven for 20 minutes until lightly golden, then remove from the oven and leave to cool on the tray for 30 minutes before transferring to a wire rack to cool completely.

The biscuits will keep well, stored in an airtight container, for up 1 week.

A delicious apple pie with strawberry jam. Cooking apples can be tart, so recipes often contain a lot of sugar to sweeten them up – this recipe uses strawberry jam to add another tasty twist. I love to serve mine with a big scoop of vanilla vegan ice cream.

Strawberry jam apple pie

SERVES 8

Vegan butter, for greasing

100g (scant ½ cup) golden caster sugar, plus 1 tbsp for sprinkling

1 tsp ground cinnamon

2 tbsp cornflour

600g (21oz) Bramley cooking apples, peeled, cored and thinly sliced

4 tbsp strawberry jam (check the label to make sure it doesn't contain gelatine – look for jams using 'fruit pectin')

500g (1lb 2oz) block vegan shortcrust pastry

Plain flour, for dusting

Vegan ice cream, to serve

Preheat the oven to 200°C/180°C Fan/400°F/gas 6 and grease a 25cm (10in) fluted tart tin (with a removable base) with vegan butter.

To make the filling, combine the sugar, cinnamon and cornflour in a large bowl. Stir in the apples, then add the strawberry jam and stir again to coat all of the apples in a thin layer of jam.

Roll out the pastry on a lightly floured surface to a thickness of 5mm (⅛in).

Line the tart tin with the pastry, trimming off any excess, then spoon in the apple slices until the mound is slightly above the edge of the tart tin.

Cut the trimmed-off pastry into 1.5cm (¾in)-wide strips, then lay the strips of pastry on top of the apple filling in a cross-hatch lattice effect and feel free to decorate the pie however you like, cutting out pastry flowers, leaves etc.

Sprinkle the pie with the extra tablespoon of sugar and bake in the centre of the oven for 45–55 minutes or golden brown all over and the apples are tender.

Remove from the oven and serve with a big scoop of vegan ice cream.

Fridge cake is a real family favourite. Watching my dad make this delicious treat was a real moment of anticipation. There was always just one question: what exactly is he going to put in it this time? Every fridge cake was different. I would urge you to do the same: if something sweet at the back of the cupboard needs using up… it goes into the mixture.

Fridge cake

MAKES 12 SLICES

100g (3½oz) unsalted vegan butter

150g (scant ½ cup) golden syrup

300g (10½oz) vegan dark chocolate, broken into pieces

200g (7oz) Biscoff biscuits, roughly broken with a rolling pin or pulsed in a food processor

60g (⅓ cup) chopped pitted dates

60g (⅓ cup) chopped dried apricots

80g (⅓ cup) roughly chopped pistachios

Large pinch of flaky sea salt

Icing sugar, for dusting (optional)

Line a 20cm (8in) square baking tin with greaseproof paper.

Put the butter and golden syrup in a saucepan and melt over a low heat, stirring gently, then add the dark chocolate and stir until it has melted and combined with the butter and syrup. Remove from the heat and add the broken biscuits, dates, apricots, pistachios and salt and stir together to mix all of the ingredients into the melted chocolate.

Tip the mixture into the lined tin and chill in the fridge for at least 3 hours.

Remove from the tin and cut the fridge cake into 12 pieces. Dust with icing sugar before serving if using.

The cake will keep well, in an airtight container in the fridge, for up to 2 weeks.

A fiery rum and ginger cake is amazing paired with a hot drink. Bringing out this treat to your guests will really start a conversation around its unique flavour. Give this a go and be ready to get asked for the recipe.

Rum and ginger cake

SERVES 8

FOR THE BATTER
160g (1⅓ cups) plain flour, sifted
1 tsp baking powder
2 tbsp ground ginger
2 tsp mixed spice
100g (generous ½ cup) brown sugar
Pinch of sea salt
150g (scant ½ cup) golden syrup
100g (3½oz) vegan unsalted butter, melted, plus extra for greasing
100ml (scant ½ cup) plant-based milk

FOR THE GLAZE
2 tbsp spiced rum
4 tbsp golden syrup

Preheat the oven to 200°C/180°C Fan/400°F/ gas 6. Grease a 2lb loaf tin and line it with greaseproof paper.

Whisk together the sifted plain flour, baking powder, ground ginger, mixed spice, brown sugar and salt in a large bowl.

Add the golden syrup, melted butter and milk to the bowl and whisk until no lumps of flour remain.

Pour the batter into the prepared tin and bake in the oven for about 30 minutes, or until a skewer inserted into the centre comes out clean.

Mix the rum and syrup together in a bowl. Remove from the oven and poke holes all over the cake with a skewer (roughly 15 holes). Pour the mixed rum and syrup over the cake, then leave to cool in the tin for 20–30 minutes. Carefully turn the cake out onto a wire rack and leave to cool completely.

The cake will keep well, stored in an airtight container, for up to 1 week.

Brownies are a magical treat that have so many variations: some are cakey, others are fudgy. I personally like a fudgy, dense brownie with chocolate chunks and a smoky roasted tahini topping. If you can't find dark roasted tahini, try using a roasted nut butter of your choice.

Dark chocolate tahini brownies

MAKES 9 BROWNIES

5 tbsp coconut oil, plus extra for greasing
200g (7oz) vegan dark chocolate, broken into pieces
100g (scant 1 cup) plain flour
1 tsp baking powder
25g (¾oz) cocoa powder
75g (⅓ cup) caster sugar
Pinch of sea salt
100ml (scant ½ cup) plant-based milk
150g (5½oz) vegan dark chocolate chunks
1 tbsp dark roasted tahini

Preheat the oven to 180°C/160°C Fan/350°F/gas 4. Grease a square baking tin (roughly 20cm/8in) with a little oil, then line it with greaseproof paper.

Melt the coconut oil in a small saucepan over a low heat, then add the chocolate pieces and keep the pan over the heat until the chocolate has melted.

Meanwhile, sift the flour, baking powder and cocoa powder into a large bowl, then stir in the sugar and salt. Stir in the oil and chocolate mix and the plant-based milk until combined. Stir in the chocolate chunks and pour the mixture into the prepared tin, spreading it out evenly. Spoon the tahini over the mixture in dollops and then swirl on top. Bake in the oven for 20 minutes until the edges are beginning to crisp up and the middle is still slightly gooey.

Remove from the oven and leave to cool for about 40 minutes, then turn out onto a wire rack to cool completely.

These brownies are best eaten fresh, but can be stored in an airtight container for up to 1 week.

I love baked cookies, but often cookie dough tastes as good as the cookies themselves. That is why I created this delicious cookie dough bar recipe, to satisfy your sweet-tooth craving straight from the fridge.

Raw cookie dough bar

MAKES 12 BARS

115g (½ cup) coconut oil, plus extra for greasing

3 tbsp smooth peanut butter

150g (¾ cup) light brown sugar

190g (1½ cups) plain flour

¼ tsp sea salt

60ml (¼ cup) plant-based milk

2 tsp vanilla extract

175g (6oz) vegan dark chocolate chips

50g (½ cup) pecans, roughly chopped

45g (½ cup) rolled oats

Melt the coconut oil and peanut butter with the brown sugar in a small saucepan over a low heat.

Mix the flour and salt in a separate mixing bowl.

Pour the coconut oil and sugar mixture into the bowl of flour, then add the milk and vanilla extract and stir to combine. Leave the mixture to cool to room temperature, then add the chocolate chips, pecans and oats and knead until evenly distributed.

Grease a square baking tin (roughly 20cm/8in) with a little oil, then press the mixture into the tin.

Chill in the fridge for about 1 hour until set, then cut into 12 squares or bars.

The cookie dough bars or squares will keep well, stored in an airtight container in the fridge, for up to 2 weeks.

Pineapple upside-down cake reminds me of a childhood spent in the kitchen watching my mum bake. She created amazing fairy cakes, delicious banana breads, profiteroles, tiramisu… the lot! But I remember the first time I watched her create a pineapple-upside down cake and it was pure magic to me.

Pineapple upside-down cake

SERVES 8

200g (1⅔ cups) self-raising flour
1 tsp baking powder
100g (scant ½ cup) caster sugar
180ml (¾ cup) plant-based milk
100g (3½oz) vegan unsalted butter, melted, plus extra for greasing
1 × 435g (15½oz) tin pineapple rings in juice (save the juice)
175g (½ cup) golden syrup

Preheat the oven to 180°C/160°C Fan/350°F/gas 4. Grease and line the base and sides of a 20cm (8in) solid round cake tin (not springform) with greaseproof paper.

Mix the flour with the baking powder and sugar in a bowl. Pour the milk, melted butter and juice from the tin of pineapple into a jug and stir to combine. Pour the liquid into the dry mix and fold together with a wooden spoon.

Pour the half cup of golden syrup into the base of the cake tin then add the pineapple rings – I usually add one full ring into the centre and then cut the other rings in half and lay them around the edges of the tin. Pour in the batter mixture and bake in the oven for 40 minutes, until the top of the sponge is golden brown.

Remove from the oven and allow to stand for at least 1 hour before removing the cake from the tin. Do this by putting a board, plate or cake stand on top of the tin and turning the board/plate/cake stand and cake tin upside down. Gently remove the tin and peel away the greaseproof paper. Cut into 8 chunky slices and serve.

Tepache is a delicious drink originating in Mexico. It utilises the pineapple skin and core to reduce waste and creates a tasty, refreshing drink for any occasion.

Tepache

MAKES 3 LITRES

300g (1½ cups) soft light
  brown sugar
1 whole, ripe fresh
  pineapple, scrubbed
  clean and peeled
1 cinnamon stick

Bring 3 litres (12½ cups) of water to the boil in a large saucepan, then turn off the heat. Add the sugar and stir to dissolve.

Put the pineapple peel, core and cinnamon stick in the pan, cover the pan with a tea towel and place on a kitchen counter or on top of a cupboard. Using a tea towel allows the mixture to 'breathe' and ferment while keeping out dust and other foreign matter. If you prefer to use a jar or tub, either remove the seal before closing the lid, or place a towel over it instead of closing the lid.

After 24 hours check your tepache for white froth on the surface. This is a sign of fermentation. If there is no froth, don't panic; simply re-cover it and leave it for another 24 hours. You can drink it now or wait for another day or two to increase fermentation, which will result in a stronger and slightly more bitter taste, and even alcoholic content.

When your tepache is ready, strain it into a jar or pitcher, squeezing the peel and core to get all of the tasty liquid out, then store in the fridge for up to a week. It will continue to slowly ferment so the taste will change over time. Compost the pineapple peel if you can.

If you haven't managed to use your bread (or slice and freeze it) before it gets stale, it seems like it's destined for the bin but don't despair – try this fruity bread pudding instead. Also check out my Bread Sauce recipe on page 36.

Fruity bread pudding

SERVES 4

2 tbsp custard powder

140g (¾ cup) light muscovado sugar

600ml (2½ cups) oat milk (shop-bought or see recipe on page 34)

500g (1lb 2oz) stale bread, cut into 1cm-(½in-) thick slices and cut into triangles

300g (10½oz) mixed fresh fruit (try using whatever berry is in season: raspberries and cherries work perfectly)

85g (3oz) chopped mixed peel (orange, grapefruit, lemon, or whatever you have)

Grated zest of 1 lemon, and lemon halved for juicing

100g (3½oz) vegan unsalted butter, melted, plus extra for greasing

Preheat the oven to 180°C/160°C Fan/350°F/gas 4 and grease a 20cm (8in) non-stick square cake tin with vegan butter.

Mix the custard powder with 1 tablespoon of the sugar in a saucepan, place over a low heat, then add 2 tablespoons of the milk and stir to form a smooth paste. Add the rest of the milk and stir, then turn up the heat and stir continuously until you have a thick, smooth custard.

Start to lay the stale bread triangles in your greased cake tin. When you have covered the base, sprinkle on some of the fruit and mixed peel, add a squeeze of lemon juice and cover with some custard. Repeat the process with more bread, fruit, lemon juice and custard until you have used all of your bread. Cover the tin with tin foil and bake in the oven for 1 hour. Remove the cover and bake for a further 30 minutes, until it is firm and the top has browned.

Remove from the oven and serve.

Spotted dick is a classic English suet sponge. This vegan version is incredibly filling and really delicious, and perfect served with hot custard. Try adding a little shot of rum to your custard for a festive feel.

Easy vegan spotted dick

SERVES 8

vegan butter, for
    greasing
250g (2 cups) self-
    raising flour
125g (4½oz) vegan suet
80g (⅓ cup) caster sugar
Grated zest of 1 lemon
Pinch of sea salt
180g (1¼ cups) raisins
200ml (generous ¾ cup)
    oat milk (shop-bought
    or see recipe on
    page 34)
Hot vegan custard,
    to serve

Grease a 15cm (6in) wide and 7cm (3in) deep pudding bowl with vegan butter.

Combine the flour and suet in a bowl and use your fingertips to rub them together to form a crumb. Add the sugar, lemon zest, salt and raisins and stir to combine. Stir in the oat milk to make a wet dough.

Transfer the mixture to the greased pudding bowl and cover with a double layer of greaseproof paper. Tie around the edge tightly with kitchen string.

Put a large saucepan (with a lid) on the hob, add the pudding bowl and fill it with enough water to come three-quarters of the way up the side of the bowl. Bring to the boil, reduce to a simmer, cover and steam for 1 hour. Top up the pan with more water if the level drops below halfway up the pudding bowl.

Carefully remove the pudding bowl from the saucepan, cut the string and remove the paper. Use a knife to ease the pudding from the sides of the bowl, then place a plate on top and invert to turn out the pudding. Serve piping hot, with custard alongside.

Tiramisu is my all-time favourite dessert! It has everything I love all in one dish: the creamy decadent layer, coffee-soaked sponge and a boozy taste. The best dessert ever created. You will need six individual small or shallow glasses.

Tiramisu

SERVES 6

FOR THE SPONGE
200g (1⅔ cups) self-raising flour
100g (scant ½ cup) caster sugar
1 tsp bicarbonate of soda
A pinch of sea salt
200ml (generous ¾ cup) plant-based milk
1 tsp vanilla extract
100g (3½oz) vegan unsalted butter, softened, plus extra for greasing

FOR THE CREAM FILLING
400g (14oz) vegan cream cheese
125ml (½ cup) plant-based milk
125ml (½ cup) amaretto liqueur (such as Disaronno)
45g (¼ cup) caster sugar

Preheat the oven to 180°C/160°C Fan/350°F/gas 4 and grease a 23cm (9in) square baking tray with butter.

To make the sponge, combine the flour with the caster sugar, bicarbonate of soda and salt.

Mix the plant-based milk and vanilla extract in a jug.

Add the vegan butter to the flour mixture and stir until it has a crumbly consistency. Add the liquid from the jug a little at a time, mixing continuously, until you have a thick, smooth batter. Pour the batter into the greased baking tray and bake in the oven for 25 minutes, until it is firm and a skewer inserted into the middle of the sponge comes out clean.

While the sponge is baking, make the cream filling. Whisk the cream cheese, milk, alcohol and caster sugar in a bowl until fully combined, then transfer to the fridge to chill.

Remove the sponge from the oven, transfer to a wire rack and leave it to cool for 1 hour, while the cream filling mixture is also chilling.

Once the sponge has cooled, cut it into 2 × 6cm (¾ x 2½in) fingers (you should get about 26 fingers).

FOR THE COFFEE

2 tbsp instant coffee
granules

2 tbsp amaretto liqueur
or bourbon

250ml (1 cup) boiling
water

FOR ASSEMBLING

50g (1¾oz) grated vegan
dark chocolate, grated

6 Amaretti biscuits,
crumbled, to serve
(optional) (shop-
bought or see recipe
on page 181)

Make the coffee for dipping the sponge by mixing the coffee granules and amaretto into the boiling water. Pour the coffee into a shallow bowl so it is easier to dip the sponge and let it cool a little before dipping.

Dip your first sponge fingers (about three fingers) in the coffee and lay them in the base of your glasses. Feel free to grate some chocolate on this layer if you are feeling decadent. Using a tablespoon, spoon the cream mixture into the glasses, then dip more sponge fingers into the coffee and lay them on top. Spoon in more cream and grate over more chocolate. Repeat the layering of soaked sponge, cream and grated chocolate until you reach the top of the glasses, finishing with the cream topped with chocolate and crumbled amaretti biscuits (if using).

Chill in the fridge for at least 30 minutes, then enjoy!

Amaretti biscuits are the perfect biscuit to enjoy with a coffee and the ultimate accompaniment crumbled on top of tiramisu (see page 177). They're so incredibly delicious and one of my favourite recipes in the whole book.

Amaretti biscuits

MAKES 12 BISCUITS

180g (2 cups) ground almonds
150g (¾ cup) caster sugar
½ tsp baking powder
75ml (⅓ cup) aquafaba (liquid from a tin of chickpeas)
½ tsp lemon juice
1 tbsp amaretto liqueur (such as Disaronno)
½ tsp vanilla or almond extract
Icing sugar, for coating

Preheat the oven to 180°C/160°C Fan/350°F/gas 4 and line a large baking tray with a piece of greaseproof paper.

Mix the ground almonds, sugar and baking powder in a large mixing bowl.

Put the aquafaba and lemon juice in a spotlessly clean bowl and whisk with an electric handheld whisk until stiff peaks form and you can turn the bowl upside down without movement in the mixture.

Gently fold a few tablespoons of the whipped aquafaba into the ground almond mixture, then gently fold in the rest. Fold in the amaretto and vanilla or almond extract. Form the mixture into 20g (¾oz) balls and roll them in icing sugar.

Place the balls on the prepared baking tray, making sure you leave enough space between them as they will spread as they bake. Dust all the balls with more icing sugar and bake in the oven for about 15 minutes, until the tops are lightly browned and cracked in places.

Remove the biscuits from the oven and leave to cool completely on a wire rack to crisp up and become less fragile.

The biscuits can be stored in an airtight jar for up to 5 days.

Treacle sponge is a truly wonderful, decadent dessert for those with the sweetest of teeth and is best served piping hot with deliciously rich custard or ice cream.

Easy vegan treacle sponge

SERVES 8

Vegan butter, for
    greasing
6 tbsp golden syrup
250g (2 cups) self-
    raising flour
125g (4½oz)vegan suet
80g (⅓ cup) caster sugar
Pinch of sea salt
200ml (generous ¾ cup)
    oat milk (shop-bought
    or see recipe on
    page 34)
Hot custard or vegan
    vanilla ice cream,
    to serve

Grease a 15cm (6in) wide and 7cm (3in) deep pudding bowl with vegan butter and spoon 4 tablespoons of the golden syrup into the bottom.

Combine the flour and suet in a bowl and use your fingertips to rub them together to form a crumb. Add the sugar and salt and stir to combine, then pour in the oat milk and mix to a wet dough.

Transfer the mixture to the greased pudding bowl and cover with a double layer of greaseproof paper. Tie around the edge tightly with kitchen string.

Put a large saucepan (with a lid) on the hob, add the pudding bowl and fill it with enough water to come three-quarters of the way up the side of the bowl. Bring to the boil, reduce to a simmer, cover and steam for 1 hour. Top up the pan with more water if the level drops below halfway up the pudding bowl.

Carefully remove the pudding bowl from the saucepan, cut the string and remove the paper. Use a knife to ease the pudding from the sides of the bowl, then place a plate on top and invert to turn out the pudding. Spoon the remaining 2 tablespoons of golden syrup over the pudding to serve.

Serve with hot custard or vanilla ice cream.

Index

BRETT COBLEY is a Chef, author, fighter of food waste and advocate for mental health. He believes that good food and conversation can change the world. Brett has been vegan for over five years and it is the best decision he ever made.

Acknowledgements

Thank you to Tebogo for putting up with me through the process of writing this book, and for being my recipe tester for all of the recipes that didn't make it. Thanks also to the team at HarperCollins for putting this book together. To Howard and Denise for helping to create such incredible shots. And to my followers and everyone reading this for all of your incredible support, it means the world to me. I am so happy to be able to bring you this book, and I cannot wait to see all of your amazing dishes posted on instagram. Don't forget to tag me **@BrettCobley**

04-06-21.

PILLGWENLLY